The Newcomer's Guide

to the

Invisible Realm:

A Journey Through
Dreams, Metaphor, and Imagination

Laura K. Deal, Ph.D.

Published by First Church of Metaphor
Copyright Laura K. Deal 2013
All Rights Reserved
ISBN-13: 978-0615847382
ISBN-10: 0615847382

Cover Design by Maia Raeder

Cover Photo by Laura K. Deal

Author Photo by Brenna Raeder

CONTENTS

Why I Wrote This Book

In March of 2009, I woke crying from this dream: *I'm standing at the counter of a hotel. My pelvis is broken in three places and there is no clerk to help me. I think, "I have to sit down," but immediately amend that to "I have to get off my pelvis." I will have to lie on the floor. The counter is now simultaneously the hotel counter and my kitchen counter. The pain is unbearable.* The dream left me shaking, and despite my experience as a dream interpreter, I couldn't figure out what it meant. Whenever I thought about the dream, the sensation of pain, instability, and unreliability in my pelvis returned, as vividly as if it had happened in waking life. The dream haunted my thoughts but I came no closer to understanding its meaning.

Six weeks later, I brought this dream to a circle of dream workers who had become my friends. The broken feeling of the dream reflected my emotional state as I sat in that circle. My mother and my mother-in-law were suffering from the illnesses that would take them both from the world within the next nine months. I'd also had pain in my hip in waking life for about five months when I had the dream. I'd never been so publicly vulnerable with my pain, but

I'd also never felt safer. It wasn't the first time I'd trusted this spiritual family with a dream.

The group offered their thoughts about the symbols and many of them made sense—the pelvis evoking motherhood, the breaks evoking grief. The fact that there was no one behind the counter suggested that there was no gatekeeper to stop me from going to this profoundly painful place. One projection in particular unleashed my tears: that I was shamanically, on a spiritual plane, helping these beloved women bear the pain they were suffering. When I got home and told my husband about the experience, he suggested that the third break in the dream could be our ancient cat, Tilki, whose weight loss and fragility echoed my mom's physical condition in profound and eerie ways. All three of these females had weakness and instability in their pelvises. The three breaks in my dream made perfect, painful sense.

Over the years, the meanings of this dream have continued to unfold for me, as just one example of the interweaving of my dream life and my waking life. As life has presented challenges, dreams have offered a mirror in which to see the larger meanings behind life's events and insight into my responses. They have offered the promise of safety even in the face of huge emotional storms, and the people who have helped me understand my dreams have held me together when I no longer had the resources to do so myself. Dreams and their meanings are essential to the fabric of my life. Without them, I would never have written this book.

Dreams have always captured my curiosity. Growing up, I tried to find answers about their meanings in books. What I really wanted was confirmation of my intuitive understanding—the knowledge that I felt in my bones—that my dreams mattered. No one in my environment encouraged this belief. Still, knowing deeply what felt true, my fascination with dreams continued into adulthood. In 2000, I met Jeremy Taylor, a dream work facilitator and Unitarian Universalist minister. In a workshop at Naropa University, he introduced about thirty of us to the "Group Projective Dream Work" method. This way of exploring dream symbols provided the safety to walk in sometimes frightening emotional territory.

That weekend proved to be the seed of a beautiful process of unfolding. Billie Ortiz also attended that workshop, and out of her engagement with dream work, she created retreats in which Jeremy could continue to share his wisdom. Like any "hero" who hears the call, I took some time away from working with Jeremy, unconsciously refusing the call, probably because I sensed the depth of dedication that answering it would require. I am forever grateful to Billie for reminding me that I might find comfort in sitting with like-minded people, addressing profound questions of the soul by exploring our dreams together. Through her Dream Retreats—we celebrated her 20th in May, 2013—I found a family of people who have seen me at my most vulnerable and held me in graceful compassion.

About a year before my dream of the broken pelvis, I sat down at a dream work retreat with Marcella Moy, a clairvoyant and intuitive reader (someone who offers clients information that she receives from the non-physical realm). I knew Marcella as part of my "dream" family. We'd shared several weekends of dream exploration and I'd seen the amazing insights she'd given to others in the process of doing dream work together. I have a great deal of trust in my own intuition, and had no reason to doubt that the information she would offer came from any place other than the Invisible Realm trying to guide me. For even longer than I'd studied dreams, I'd been writing fiction with an eye to getting my creative work published. So whenever I sat with an intuitive reader, the questions of "Am I on the right path?" and, "Will this current book be the one that 'makes' it?" were always on my mind.

"Yes," Marcella told me. "You'll get some books published. The one that you really need to write, though, is about all this." Her gesture included her desk as well as the room where our dream circle would gather in a few hours. "An introduction to dreams, yes, but more than that. Intuition and readings and all of it."

I'd never considered writing such a book before.

After that reading, I couldn't stop thinking about it. At first, all the reasons why I shouldn't cropped up. This is a common phase in many creative projects, but I listened to the voices that whispered, "People will think you're crazy," and "You can't prove any of it."

I listened, but I didn't let the voices stop me. Because I've seen how much dream work can help people understand themselves and make it easier to live in a complicated world. Because I've had powerful moments where intuition saved me from small inconveniences and larger disasters. Because I've found comfort in the meditative quality of reading the Tarot, and because I've had visits from ghosts when I've written ghost stories. Too much of my life is lived in the Invisible Realm to deny its existence.

I worked on the book in fits and starts, interrupted by the deaths of my mother and my mother-in-law, and the profound grieving that ensued. During that time my dreams brought me comfort, but even more importantly, the communities of dreamers and writers with whom I work provided safe places to be fully present with my grief. After nearly a year, the dreams that I brought to my dream groups became insistent in their message: "You've been given work to do. Now is the time to do it." So I returned to the writing of this book, in the hopes that it might make the Invisible Realm easier to access for those whose upbringings or communities have rationalized it away, and to reassure those who have already started along this road that they aren't alone.

The rationalist viewpoint is deeply ingrained in modern Western culture, and as the daughter of two atheists with scientific leanings, it has formed my world view as well. I understand the need for scientific inquiry and the creative thrust toward technological innovation, and I enjoy the fruits of our greater rational understanding and clever inventions every day. I appreciate that machines give me more leisure time in which to pursue my passions. I would likely have died of appendicitis without medical advances that made appendectomies routine and generally safe. A clever suction-cup gadget helped deliver my first baby, without which things might have taken a very dangerous turn. So I don't reject the rationalist, materialist, scientific viewpoint. But there hasn't been enough research on the powers of the mind to widen that viewpoint to include intuition and telepathy and the meanings of dreams.

As a species, we've had a long and precipitous growth in technological innovation over the last few hundred years. In my grandmother's lifetime, cars, telephones, and air travel grew from infancy to mainstays of society. She lived through the golden age of radio, the invention of television, electric typewriters, personal computers, camcorders, digital cameras, and the birth of the Internet. All that technical innovation has its dark side. My grandmother also lived through two world wars, the Great Depression, the Cold War, and the threat of atomic and nuclear destruction.

The mental strain of living in a world that is changing faster than ever before is a huge challenge for humans. As living organisms, we respond to stresses in our environment in an attempt to adapt. The urge toward survival drives us to find ways to cope with emotional stress as well as physical. Some turn to religion and spirituality, some to sedatives and tranquilizers, some to art. Others crack under the strain and suffer mental and physical illness, or commit violence against others or themselves. If we want to heal the violent and ill among us, we must first confront the potential for violence and illness within our own psyches. By becoming more aware of our own capacity to do the very things we see as evil and sick, the more we understand that "There, but for the grace of God, go I." Seeing ourselves honestly builds empathy, just as participating in dream work or reading a vibrant story deepens our understanding of other viewpoints.

I wrote this book because through the course of my studies and explorations, I've become convinced that embracing the wisdom and compassion offered in the Invisible Realm is the surest way to pull ourselves back from the brink of outrunning our spiritual growth with the pace of innovation, and destroying our habitat in the process. Not that change itself is bad, but if we keep speeding up, keep expanding our networks, our attention will become so fragmented we'll lose sight of the whole—both the whole of society, and the whole being within. In order to cope with change, we need to move forward consciously, and tapping into the river of awareness in the Invisible Realm is the best way I've found to become conscious.

The journey needs to be a path toward wholeness. As children in a rapidly changing world, we fractured and compartmentalized behaviors and beliefs that didn't accord with those around us. We learned to restrain our impulses and emotions in an effort to conform to the norms modeled by family and school and society. These essential survival mechanisms have, like everything, a shadow side, which we must recognize and acknowledge later in life so that the shadow doesn't eat away at us from within. As adults, it becomes just as urgent to our survival to rediscover the talents, especially intuitive and creative abilities, that we might have shut down as children because they weren't taught in our schools, or homes, or anywhere. A natural gift might have even been derided as foolishness or worse, squelched with physical violence. Yet that gift will be the one that we must embrace. Reintegration of those abandoned parts of ourselves is the path toward spiritual health, which flows into emotional and physical health.

We can find those parts of ourselves in the Invisible Realm.

Part One:

What Is the Invisible Realm?

Living a life of meaning includes frequent travel into the Invisible Realm, but what exactly is it, and how do we get there? The short answer is: It's where we live. There aren't truly newcomers to the Invisible Realm, for all of us live there every day. But much of our habits of mind and behavior aren't fully conscious, especially when we get caught up in moments of tension, or old patterns. The Invisible Realm unfolds before our imaginations when we notice it, when we pay attention. The light of focused awareness will be our lantern as we explore this strange land all around us.

If you ask me where I live, I might answer with a street address, a neighborhood, a town, or state, or country. I might say "I live in my office," meaning I work too much, or "I live in my car," meaning I spend a lot of time commuting. Whatever my answer, I'll probably tell you where my physical body resides.

But what about my mental, emotional, body? My mind can take my thoughts and awareness far away from my body at any time.

I might remember the time when I was seven, and got a call before school to hurry next door to see my best friend's cat birthing kittens. I can picture myself crouching beside the cardboard box lined with an old blanket. I can see Meekay's black-dominated, calico coat, and remember her washing the amniotic sac off her newborn.

Remembering this takes the focus of my awareness away from my physical surroundings and into the Invisible Realm. I can easily switch to more immediate awareness, as I pause to look up a word in the dictionary or hear a sound that my mind wants to identify. We live in the Invisible Realm when we dream or daydream and our imaginations take over. We live there when we anticipate the future or dwell on the past, or lose ourselves in a novel. When we brainstorm solutions to problems we tap into association and imagination, two important aspects of the Invisible Realm. When anxieties overtake us, or we escape into a creative flow, we experience the power of the Invisible Realm.

Another answer to the question "What is the Invisible Realm?" is that it's where we avoid going. This sounds completely counter to the answer above. How can it be both "Where I live" and "Where I avoid going"? The nature of the Invisible Realm, however, is that it thrives in paradox. Both apparently contradictory statements can be true. I live in my imagination, my perception of what's happening around me. Yet I can also avoid paying attention to the subconscious motivations that make me choose what I choose for myself. People often find life-partners who fulfill their expectations of how they deserve to be treated. If a woman's father died when she was a baby, for instance, her life experience is that the most important man in her life will be unavailable to her. If she doesn't consciously work through this childhood expectation, she may marry a man who is emotionally unavailable.

Or if something happened long ago that is too painful to think about, my conscious mind turns away from reminders of that event. Yet the memory, however deeply suppressed, lives on within me, and might be triggered unexpectedly. Simple triggers can send people suffering from post-traumatic stress disorder into the same physical and mental responses they experienced at the time of the original trauma. It's worth becoming aware of these hidden places within ourselves so our reactions can be more conscious and creative rather than merely primal.

This sounds like the province of psychoanalysis, and it certainly can be. If your problems feel overwhelming, or if distressing information arises as you begin to explore, please do seek the help of a professional counselor. But you can pursue deeper self-understanding and healing on your own, or with the help of loved ones and friends. I discuss some of those paths more fully in later chapters.

The Invisible Realm also encompasses such mysteries as the origins of the universe. Scientists use the language of mathematics to talk about it, while humans traditionally have used metaphors to explain how everything started. In my understanding, it doesn't matter what metaphor we use to describe the origins of our universe as long as we recognize that our words are too limited to fully encompass what we intend to describe. The "Big Bang" is one metaphor, arising from a scientific approach to explaining how we as humans in our vast universe came to be. To me, Genesis 1:1 in the Old Testament expresses the same idea, in a pre-technological, intuitive way: "In the beginning God created the heavens and the earth." Both of these metaphors conjure for me the image of the creation of our universe which unleashed the energetic and physical unfolding that continues on forever, as far as we can tell. And we're a part of that unfolding, waves in the ocean of divine creative energy.

We experience the world physically, dwelling in a tangible environment that we understand with the traditional five senses of the body: touch, taste, smell, sight, and hearing. We also experience it energetically, in our emotions and intuition and imagination. If we can remember that we are expressions of divine energy, made in the creative likeness of that divine energy, it's easier to navigate life's storms and difficulties.

How Do I See It if It's Invisible?

We perceive the Invisible Realm with the inner eye, or imagination, and through such physical sensations as chills or the hair rising on the backs of our necks. The many ways of bringing the Invisible Realm to light deal in approximations and symbols. When I travel to another country, I can take photographs, keep a travel journal or sketch book, make a movie of the entire trip, and bring back souvenirs, but I can't fully provide another person with my experience. Even two people traveling to all the same places at the same time will have different experiences, shaded by an entire life's worth of memories and expectations that each brings to the new moment.

So it is when we report on our journeys to the Invisible Realm. An artist's image or sculpture, a writer's story or essay, a composer's music—each of these is only an approximation of the original inspiration that came from the Invisible Realm. I can tell a dream, including every minute detail from the texture of the clothing to the intensity of the light, and everyone who hears my report will imagine that dream for herself or himself. Even my report is only an approximation of the experience of the dream—a memory of it—and my telling of how my heart pounded is a different sensation than my heart actually pounding.

So we can glimpse the Invisible Realm for ourselves, but in order to show it to others we must hold up some filter of words or images or sounds or smells, and each of the filters brings its own distortion. Does this make it untruthful? Not useful?

On the contrary. Every report from the Invisible Realm invites the hearer to imagine the realm for herself. Every artwork or performance or book allows the audience member or reader to glimpse her own version of the vision the artist was trying to capture. Every time a person engages with another person's experience of the Invisible Realm, she enters that realm herself, though the use of her imagination.

Definitions

In order to communicate, we'll need to agree on some definitions.

First, when discussing the interpretation of dream symbols and the exploration of a dream's meaning, I will use the phrases "dream work" and "dream reading" interchangeably. Jeremy Taylor uses the phrase "dream work," evoking the sense of something we work as we might work in wood or words to create something new. In "working" a dream we explore the various meanings of the symbols and how they relate to each other and to the dreamer's waking life. I have come to prefer the phrase "dream reading," however, because "reading" carries with it the association of reading a book or poem (to which the reader brings her own understandings that will shape her interpretation of the story's meaning), and the "New Age" sense of a clairvoyant or intuitive reader (who might "read" palms, or cards, or astrological charts) who brings both his knowledge of the traditional meanings of what he's interpreting as well as his own intuitive understanding of what the symbols might mean for his client. While "dream work" and "dream reading" thus carry different connotations, the process of dream exploration that they describe is the same.

Second, the English language is woefully inadequate in its lack of a gender neutral singular pronoun. I will use "he" and "she" interchangeably when discussing hypothetical individuals in the examples provided. No sexism is intended.

Third, and most importantly, in talking about the Invisible Realm, one can't long avoid bringing up God. However, what I mean by God and what someone else means by God might be very different. For that reason, I tend to use other words, like "Divine" or the "Creative Energy of the Universe" or even simply, "Universe." My own experience tells me that what I perceive as "God" is truly beyond human language to describe or grasp. It is that life and love which permeates everything, both the animate and the inanimate. It is the energy unleashed by the Big Bang, and the great mystery of love. "God" does not, in this book, refer to the deity of any particular faith, but to the Mystery behind all religious constructs of understanding.

No matter how we try to explain the vast universe, the heavens and space that surround us, we arrive at the unanswerable questions, the Unnameable Mystery. What was before the Big Bang? Considering this question challenges my beliefs and understanding about time and causality: How could there be a "before" if the Big Bang was the beginning, yet how could everything have arisen out of nothing?

The Big Bang sounds a lot like the ancient creation myths that are found throughout human cultures: God, whether masculine or feminine or animal, created Earth out of the void. We use metaphors to try to grasp concepts beyond words. "The Unnameable, All That Is, Energy of the Universe" is a bit clunky, but comes close to my understanding of what I'm trying to convey.

Why Visit the Invisible Realm?

When we consciously visit the Invisible Realm we enrich our daily experience. We can more easily choose our own actions, and we can learn to relate to others with more compassion as we gain honest understanding of our own motivations. Throughout history, people have sought the experience of the Invisible Realm through creative acts, prayer, storytelling, and sharing dreams. In our modern, rationalist culture, our focus has been on clever invention, rather than on wise involvement with the world.

Teens, especially, seem to yearn for an understanding of the Invisible Realm. While children are often close to it, by the time they reach their teens, they have learned a lot from their societies and families about what is "real" and acceptable, and have often learned to subdue their own talents and intuitions quite effectively. But as the imperative of the teen years grows stronger—to separate from the parents and find one's own path—so the yearning for the understanding of the self grows. And part of that understanding is the knowledge, sometimes unconscious, that there is more to life than the body.

Many people turn to mind-altering experiences like drinking alcohol or smoking marijuana to find that space that is different from their day-to-day experiences. These substances can become a substitute for a deeper spiritual connection. Other people look for spiritual connection in religion, becoming born again or fundamentalist or converting to a new faith altogether. For some, this sets them on a lifelong path of faith and community that proves to be healthy and enduring. For others, it's a flash of intensity that burns out and leaves them searching anew months or years later. It's important, therefore, to be aware of the many avenues available to access the Invisible Realm, which is never further away than our focused awareness.

Whatever a person's prior experience, visiting the Invisible Realm is a way to increase compassion and understanding, and to bring deeper meaning to life.

Deepening Compassion

Billie Ortiz, a skilled and dedicated Dream Work Facilitator, views her work as her spiritual practice, as do all the dedicated dream readers that I know. The work is so important, she will explain, because as a culture, we've become too literal, and have lost much of our ability to think in metaphor. When we do that, we lose our imagination, and when we lose our imagination, we lose our compassion, because we can't imagine ourselves as someone else or imagine someone else's experience.

Without compassion, it's much too easy to slide into scapegoating and violence. Without compassion, we are quick to judge, but, if we understand what pain another person carries, we are more inclined to accept. The potential for disaster is great—we have the evidence of the Holocaust and, depressingly, any number of other genocides and wars. In order to heal, to live peacefully beside our neighbors, we must reawaken compassion in our lives.

Many spiritual practices express the belief that to heal the outer world, we must first heal ourselves. Compassion for yourself can be even harder than compassion for another if you've been raised to be self-critical. Dream reading leads to understanding the self, which frequently leads to compassion for the self. Old patterns can be hard to change, and self-critical "tapes" that play in our heads can be the hardest to replace. Of course, dream reading isn't the only path, but in my experience, it's the fastest and most rewarding.

At a children's writers and illustrators conference in 2010, I had the pleasure of hearing Bruce Coville, an author, speak. He believes fiction is vital to children's development because it allows them to enter into other points of view and understand how someone else might think. It raises their ability to feel compassion.

This is true for adults as well. Both dreams and fiction speak in metaphorical language, even if the fiction seems just like real life. Deeply woven into a novel's fabric is a theme, expressed through the particulars of the story. While details of plot and character will differ significantly from a reader's own experience, a story will resonate with the reader when the theme is one that the reader has grappled with (unconsciously or consciously). If the theme isn't familiar to the reader, the story allows her to journey safely into unfamiliar territory, and offers a possible road map for situations that might arise later in life. In that sense, the story itself is a metaphor for a particular facet of human experience.

Making Life Meaningful

I recently had the chance to listen to an older relative tell family stories about his brother, his parents, grandparents and other relatives. All of us who listened were acutely aware that he is our last link with those stories, those memories that live on in his mind. As he told the stories, each listener's imagination filled in details, images, and new understandings of family patterns. We saw how experience molded these ancestors, and how that shaped the generations that followed. My husband and I gained insights into his family of origin that reshaped our interpretation of past events.

This ancestor lost her self-confidence when her sister blossomed. That grandmother was in pain and her suffering made her seem unwelcoming. This one's father told him he should be able to control his body's ailments. This one was abused, but never told anyone out of crippling shame. This one's father died and he had to take a job at sixteen to support his mother. That one's father died when she was young, and she never could trust that she was safe in the world. The perception by a child, or a new in-law, of behavior as perplexing or even hurtful, suddenly shifts to understanding and compassion when we see the reason behind that behavior.

All of these wounds, and many more like them, shaped our ancestors and so shaped us. By understanding those patterns, we can make better decisions about our own behaviors, and grow our compassion for those around us. No one gets through life unscathed.

No matter how people deal with their experiences, there are painful moments in their past. If I can remember that, I'm less likely to take offense when someone snaps at me, or tries to be funny in a way that is a put-down, or says something offhand that feels aggressive. It can help me remain calm, and view the situation with understanding, so that I don't take on the moment as another injury.

Understanding family patterns also makes it possible to choose those that work, and change those that don't. When I married my husband, I had only an inkling of how generous, kind, and connected his extended family is. It still seems rare to me that all the cousins and second cousins would get along, given their various careers and interests. It seems so, because my family didn't make a big effort to get together with cousins, or to keep in touch other than by the occasional phone calls and holiday cards with aunts and uncles. So my husband's family pattern of staying connected, of making an effort to remain friends, appeals to me and makes me want to adopt that pattern over mine to hand down to my children.

In the Invisible Realm, we are waves in and of the creative ocean of the universe. We are contained in love beyond under-standing. The great spiritual teachers of the world all invite us to consider a higher perspective, but it's easy to get caught up in our individual perspective and see ourselves as separate from the divine, from the creative energy of the universe. Staying consciously aware of the Invisible Realm allows us find some comfort in the struggles of life, and can even sometimes lessen those struggles as we make more conscious choices of how to live our lives.

Preparing the Vessel

In order to travel anywhere, we need a vessel to travel in. That vessel may be as basic as our own bodies, putting one foot in front of the other, or as complicated as a space ship to take us to distant planets. Getting to the Invisible Realm requires a different sort of vessel, though our bodies are certainly a part of it. Imagination is the organ that enables us to perceive the Invisible Realm, and the more we access imagination, the easier it is to make the trip. Or, to be more precise, to make the trip with conscious awareness, because in truth, we live there all the time.

If I'm going to travel in the physical world, I need to have a vehicle and a direction. Whether I walk around the block or fly overseas, I have to move from one place to the next. If I'm walking, my body needs to have a basic level of ability. If I'm driving, my car needs to have wheels and a motor. If I'm going to visit the Invisible Realm with intention and awareness, I need to exercise my attention and imagination. I have to prepare my vehicle, or vessel, so that I can visit the Invisible Realm and receive information from it.

The first requirement is curiosity. I remember being a kid and lying on the grass in my backyard, staring up at the rich blue sky, wondering why I was me and not somebody else. Why the daughter of a couple of mathematicians with a comfortable house and food for the table rather than a poor kid in some other country on the other side of the world? I wondered why I was born then, and not a hundred years earlier. I wondered if I'd have still been *me* if my parents had married other people and I'd been born to a different set of parents. The great mysteries of life have created religions and philosophies and world views, but they remain, ultimately, mysteries. I still ponder those questions from time to time, but I've also come to accept that the mysteries are too large for me to grasp, and that all I can hope to do is to understand some little pieces of them.

As I got older, my curiosity turned to my dreams. I still remember a few dreams I had when I was in preschool, and the recurring nightmare I had well into my teens. At some point in my teen years I began writing down dreams that struck me as particularly interesting, but I didn't begin to keep a dedicated dream diary until my thirties. Some dreams from my teens and twenties stand out as clearly as waking life memories, and I knew, intuitively, that dreams held keys to parts of the mystery of who I was and why I behaved and believed the way I did.

That desire to understand myself also drove me to keep a waking life journal. In those pages, I wrestled with my emotional life—what made me happy and what made me miserable, why I loved the people I loved and why I avoided others. It was all part of paying attention.

Once I became a mother, I needed to start paying better attention to the things that made me upset. I wanted to be a calm parent, able to deal with temper tantrums and crises with equanimity. This, of course, became an ongoing struggle, as my kids pushed buttons I didn't even know I had, awakening leftover tensions and upsets from my own childhood. Paying attention has helped me to understand those triggers, and sometimes, to notice what's upsetting me before my emotions escalate. A friend of mine had struggled with his teenage son's intensifying moods and anger. One night, he dreamed that he stood in his kitchen with huge push buttons on his chest and belly. As his son started yelling at him, my friend disconnected the buttons. When he woke, he realized that he didn't need to let his son's anger upset him so, and the image of disconnecting the buttons helped him stay calm as he moved through the following days.

Paying attention to dreams can yield such immediate and satisfying results, but often the messages are harder to interpret. For a couple of years, while my daughter struggled with constant digestive trouble, I dreamed almost every night that she and I were together in whatever situation the dreams presented. She might not be an active participant in the dream, but I would notice her presence and write it in my dream journal in the morning. Finally, in waking life, her doctor suggested that gluten sensitivity might be the source of her trouble, and since there was autoimmune disease on my side of the family, might also be a problem for me. She and I went on a gluten-free diet, which helped us both dramatically and almost immediately. After that, she stopped appearing so consistently in my dreams. As I understand it now, the dreams in which she appeared were trying to tell me that she and I had the same problem, and once I addressed that problem, the urgent need for me to notice her condition vanished.

Paying Attention to Emotions

One of the best ways to prepare for a thorough journey into the Invisible Realm is to pay attention to our own emotions and the meanings we ascribe to patterns and synchronicities in our lives. One night when I was writing this book I heard the Billy Joel song "Vienna Waits For You" at a high school musical performance. It took me back to my own years in high school, and the lyrics stayed in my head. "If you're so smart, tell me why are you still so afraid?" and "You can get what you want or you can just get old."

Fear is a patterned response to the world, one I learned in the womb, I'm sure. I learned to worry from early childhood on, and I had such high-wired anxiety in pre-school and grade school that the family doctor prescribed sedatives. I'm afraid of strange things, like computer crashes and malfunctions and letting go of stuff, but not, for instance, common fears like spiders and public speaking. I know I've taught myself to get over my fears of spiders and bees through conscious processes of my mind—a skill learned in the Invisible Realm that I strive to apply to the things that still trigger me.

To work with it, I use a variation on a visualization that Natalie Sudman, a gifted intuitive reader, offered me for increasing my intuition. I picture my fear as a circle, beside my love, and I imagine the fear shrinking to a smaller circle while imagining the circle of love getting bigger. And, if I can't feel that love for whatever reason, I imagine the circle as my courage. Just keep showing up. That's really the only choice for the traveler to the Invisible Realm. Once you've glimpsed the way, your psyche will urge your ego to follow, even if the path is only visible one moment at a time. I've learned to show up in the moment and ask myself, "What lies before me now?" Creative work? Rest? Meditation? Whatever it is, fear doesn't need to come along.

This is one of the most important things I've learned about living my life: Show up and do it anyway. Show up and do it no matter how I feel about doing it. It can be hard to distinguish between a reluctance borne of the need to rest and reluctance because of fear. I try to rest first, and then show up and face it, whatever it is, from a story problem to my own shadows. If I don't, my dreams, and sometimes my life, will remind me that I have work to do.

Paying Attention to Synchronicities

Carl Jung coined the term "synchronicity" to refer to what he saw as meaningful coincidences. He offers the example of clocks that stop the moment of their owner's death. As he says, "It often seems that even inanimate objects co-operate with the unconscious in the arrangement of symbolic patterns."[1] When a dreamer sees something in waking life that connects to another outer event or an

---

[1] Jung, *Man and His Symbols*, p. 41.

inner event, that's synchronicity. It serves to focus the mind on the symbolic meaning that connects the two events.

In my experience, synchronicities tend to occur most frequently when I'm deep in discussions of dreams or the study of fairy tales, or just puzzling over some aspect of my life from the perspective of the Invisible Realm. As I have paid attention to synchronicities, I've learned more and more about myself. Sometimes the synchronicities are impossible to ignore. After studying dream work for several years with Jeremy Taylor, I entered the certification program he offers through the Marin Institute for Projective Dream Work. As part of the program, I needed to explore non-Western approaches to dream work, and so I signed up for a workshop offered by Robert Moss, another man who has devoted his life to understanding the dream world, but from an Aboriginal and shamanic perspective rather than from a primarily symbolic and Jungian perspective.

The workshop met at a retreat center on the East coast. On the second day, I participated in a group effort to obtain information from the Invisible Realm. In a group of four, we took turns being the "target," or the "questioner," that is, the person who would hold a question in mind, without telling the other three what the question was. As Robert Moss drummed, the other three in the group imagined two ravens, Thought and Memory, guiding us, showing us what we needed to see. Having had a writing practice for many years, it was easy for me to follow the scenes that unfolded before my inner eye. In one of the four trances, I flew with my ravens over a vast forest, to a cleared circle in the woods. I saw the questioner as a group leader, and then I saw an interconnected web of roots beneath the ground that made me think of aspen trees. I realized the aspen image was a metaphor for how this group would grow into many groups. The purpose of the groups was to bring people into nature to work with dreams. Then I saw the questioner traveling, helping elephants and bears, and writing. In my vision, he walked a tightrope and fell, but the ravens caught him, and then before him lay a clear road.

After the trance, the three of us who had journeyed on the questioner's behalf shared our reports. One woman dreamed of vast acres of land, and a center created by the questioner for the purpose of bringing a lot of creative endeavors together. The other woman saw a retreat center and trees, among other things. When we'd all shared our visions, the questioner told us that his cherished hope was to create a retreat center, perhaps in Germany's Black Forest, where he would lead people in music, dream exploration, and other creative pursuits.

The experience affirmed for me that such "imagined" journeys can indeed access information in ways that a rationalistic, scientific world view does not recognize. I don't know whether the three of us had a premonition of the questioner's future, or whether we glimpsed the structure of his waking dream telepathically. But I do know that we reflected back to him a beautiful possibility for his life, and reinforced his calling.

For me, the strong similarities between our visions gave credence to Robert Moss's shamanic approach to dreams and visions. It made me more inclined to accept Robert's assertions that dreams should be examined for literal meanings in the form of premonitions. I struggled to reconcile the different views on the Invisible Realm offered by Jeremy Taylor and Robert Moss, two men who had each studied dreams for decades and had come to different understandings of the primary function of dreams. How could each be right?

As I walked on the beach that evening, I noticed a float from a fishing net or boat. It had washed up on the beach, with the lettering "Taylormade" clearly visible. It took me a few moments to realize that the float's words were a synchronous message from the universe. I'd formed my understanding on Jeremy's Taylor's teachings, and was bringing that framework of understanding to the shamanistic side of the work. I dreamed that night that I was at the retreat center and Jeremy Taylor had arrived and was walking toward me, with the intention of resolving the differences of opinion with Robert Moss. When I woke, I understood something that I'd heard Jeremy say many times: "I know it's true, and it's much too important for you to take my word for it." Until that moment, I didn't get it, deep in my gut, that the only thing I can know is what I've experienced or understood for myself. Believing anyone else, without testing their experiences against my own, is giving away my power to travel the Invisible Realm. It's like looking at the photos and hearing the traveler's tales of those who have gone before, rather than visiting those places myself.

Paying Attention to Meaning and 'Ahas'

In dream reading, I recognize that only the original dreamer can say what his or her dream means. The touchstone for this is the "aha" feeling of recognition that the dreamer has when hearing something true about the dream. For those people who spend a lot of time in analytical thought, the response might get expressed in words: "That's interesting." Spontaneous laughter and sudden coughing are fairly reliable indicators that the work has touched something true for the dreamer.

But more often, the response is a more subtle physical sensation. Bodies provide a lot of intuitive knowledge. It takes paying attention to signals like tingles, chills, or shivers. I learned long ago that when something feels deeply true, I get chills on my arms, scalp, and back. This knowledge came in handy when I started participating in dream groups. Billie Ortiz calls it the "tingle test." When we reach a metaphorical understanding of a dream and the insight is accompanied by a chill or a tingle, it's our intuition offering the confirmation that we've touched on something true in the Invisible Realm. For me, and for a number of my friends who regularly read dreams, such an intuitive "aha" also accompanies the telling of stories from waking life, especially when the stories touch on synchronicities and non-physical ways of knowing or healing. Sometimes, these chills give me a better sense of my energy body around my physical one, as I perceive the sensation originating outside the boundary of my skin.

In trusting my own experience, I see meaning in events that others might consider coincidental or just chance. By choosing to search for and see meaning, my life becomes more meaningful. And the older I get, the more convinced I am that to live life without seeing any meaning in it is to live a very bleak existence indeed.

As humans, we're designed to look for patterns and to construct meaning out of the world around us. By paying attention to small and large events, I've come to understand some of the cues. When I have a really good idea, my scalp will tingle. I like to think of this as my guidance alerting me to pay attention. If I hear something three times from three different people, I also pay close attention. I suppose that's in part because three is the archetypal number of fairy tales, so it has a deep cultural resonance. The example that comes to mind is when I taught writing classes to kids and in one week three women asked, "When are you going to offer writing classes for adults?" By the third time I heard the question, the idea had taken root and the classes I subsequently offered for adults were delightful experiences.

I understand the risks of relying on signs and portents, especially because, as a fallible human being, I could easily read them wrong. I've had my intuition clouded by hope and expectation, and I try to learn from such experiences to notice the difference between true intuitive understanding and ego-driven desire. A woman I know suffers from mild paranoia, so whenever she overhears a conversation (usually not clearly because she's a little deaf) she assumes that the people are saying mean things about her. She assigns meaning that no one else would, and assumes the worst. I try to work from the assumption that my unseen guidance is trying to assist me. Someone once said that if the universe can't get our attention with a feather, it will use a brick. I try always to notice the feathers so that the brick isn't necessary.

A couple of months after my mother died, when I was still deep in valleys of grief, I got my bicycle out to go for a ride but stopped for a moment beside my garden. When I put my hand back on the handlebar, I didn't see the honeybee that had landed there, and it stung my palm. I love bees, and regretted the creature's death, and fortunately didn't suffer greatly from the sting, though the injury remained visible for weeks afterward. Six weeks later, I saw an acupuncturist, and out of curiosity, I asked him if the sting site (which was still red) had any relevance in acupuncture. He told me it was where he'd place a needle to activate Pericardium 8, the protection of the physical and emotional heart. Since bees represented for me my first success at publishing my fiction (with "The Silent Meadow," a story about bees, among other things), I chose to assign meaning to that sting: my work would protect my heart from the grief that life offered. I needed that reminder at the time, and sometimes I still forget. It's true, though, that writing sustains me through the bad times when nothing else seems to help. I'd rather see the bee sting as carrying that meaning than just have it be another random event in my life. The meaning I perceived in that bee sting helped to lift me out of my grief.

The Language of Metaphor

One of the hardest things about traveling in a foreign country is not understanding spoken or written speech. Even when the basic language is the same, different locations will have different idioms and accents that can make it challenging to engage in conversation. The language spoken in the Invisible Realm is that of metaphor. It's easiest to see in dream reading, so I'll talk about that here, and there's a lot more about dreams later in the Guide.

In school, we learn that a metaphor is a literary device like a simile, in which one thing stands for another. In other words, a symbol. It's not a great leap to go from the literary definition to interpreting dream symbols in metaphorical ways, and yet this step can be difficult for those of us raised in a rationalist society. It's hard to grasp that when I dream of death, the dream does not (usually) indicate a portent of literal death, but rather a profound transformation. Death stands as a symbol for some part of my psyche or being that is changing so dramatically that only death serves as an adequate metaphor. Dreams speak in the language of symbols because symbols can convey many meanings, and so a dream can carry several messages for the dreamer that would be lost if the only level of understanding were a literal one. Not that dreams can't be literal, or obvious, but even literal dreams have layers of symbolic meanings.

I've studied dream symbols and explored their meanings for most of my life, but more seriously since the year 2000. One of the most important things I've learned is that dream symbols have universal meanings. I practice a style of dream reading that was pioneered and popularized by Jeremy Taylor, which is commonly known as Projective Dream Work. A better name might be Consciously Projective Dream Work, because people consciously admit ownership of their projections onto other people's dreams. For example, if Nancy tells me a dream about wrestling a snake, when I hear the dream I can't help but imagine the scenes and situations for myself. Then the only things that I can suggest about the meanings of the dream will be those that are true for me. "In my imagined version of this dream," I might say, "the snake represents transformation, because snakes are known for shedding their skins. Since I'm wrestling with the snake, I'm struggling with a transformation that I'm undergoing." For Nancy, this may or may not have resonance; if she has an "aha" moment, or chills, or a strong emotional reaction, these are good signs that my projection has touched the truth of the dream for her.

Dreamers I've worked with have often been blown away by the accuracy of the projections they hear from others in a group. While it's true that some dream workers have more experience and a deeper understanding of symbolic language than others, it's also true that the accuracy arises precisely because symbols carry universal meanings. The accuracy isn't because the projections are what the dreamer wants to hear, but generally the opposite: the "ahas" the dreamer has can make her aware of uncomfortable truths, but the awareness leads to healing.

Even when the native tongues differ, the symbols resonate in similar ways. We find this too in the universality of fairy tale themes. Jeremy Taylor explores a number of the cross-cultural motifs in *The Living Labyrinth.* Tales of enchanted frogs, for example, show up with local variations in Europe, Russia, China, India, Africa, and in Native American and Pacific Island traditions.[2] The fact that cultures all over the world have tales of enchanted frogs suggests that the symbolism of the frog carries universal meanings.

This universality of metaphor and symbolic language is what made me realize that dream work is a spiritual practice. By speaking in this common language, we discover the ways in which we are alike. By consciously owning my projections on someone else's dream, I admit to myself that there are parts of my psyche that look very much like the parts of someone else's psyche. That admission creates compassion. Not pity, which takes a superior attitude, but true compassion, in which I can fully understand how someone else feels, or why they acted the way they did, or that there are parts in each of us that feel too scary to look at, much less own.

In addition to the dreams we experience while sleeping, we use metaphor to wrap our thoughts around concepts and ideas that are difficult to grasp, like God, or creation, or profound emotion. Sometimes the metaphor takes the shape of spoken and written language, but other times it speaks through music, or art. When a

---

[2] Taylor, *The Living Labyrinth*, pp. 15-31.

photographer frames the perfect shot, we say he or she has a good eye, meaning that the photograph evokes an emotional or spiritual reaction that is hard to put into words. The best art is art we can hang our own projections on, thereby understanding, or even just experiencing, something of ourselves that we hadn't known before.

We aren't, as a rule, raised to think in symbolic terms. Modern society tends toward rationalistic, scientific thinking, dismissing experiences that can't be replicated and studied, such as intuitive knowledge and spiritual connection. The appellation of "dreamer" is not generally a compliment. And yet, by adhering strictly to this literal, scientific view, we run the risk of losing touch with an essential part of our being. Our dreams come to help us find that connection again, if only we pay attention and make an effort to speak the language.

For some, learning the language will take a while, but that doesn't mean it's not worth learning. Recently, a friend who speaks several languages fluently expressed her unhappiness at not being able to learn the language of metaphor very well. She'd been working dreams with friends for a long time, but felt she hadn't mastered the art of projecting onto dreams, of seeing the dream images as symbols. When I imagine having this feeling, it's because I'm reluctant to face what my psyche wants to show me through dream reading.

It's true that it can be overwhelming at first to see dreams and the waking world as a great cauldron of metaphor. We're taught, at least in "rational" and technology-based cultures, to view the world in a mechanistic, logical way. And the waking world generally provides consistency that encourages that view. If I leave a book-mark in a book when I go to sleep, I don't expect that when I wake it will be in a different place. Viewing the world as reliably consistent is probably crucial to our sanity. When we go to the grocery store, we pretty much know what to expect. If my roses always bloom yellow, I'd be astonished to have them bloom red.

Yet overlying this view of the world, we can also learn to see the symbols and significance that synchronicities and unusual moments provide for us. I'd been struggling for a few weeks with the question of whether my chosen career path really made any sense, when I saw a man in the grocery store with a prosthetic leg. The day was warm, so he wore shorts, and his leg was not designed to look like a human leg, but only to behave like one. The sight struck me as unusual, but I didn't think any more about it, until five minutes later at the other end of the store, I saw a man, also wearing shorts, with two prosthetic legs. At that point I asked myself what message I should take from this odd coincidence. After all, it had been years since I'd seen a man in the grocery store with a visible prosthetic leg.

As a metaphor, I'd have to look at the symbol from a couple of angles. One is that I might be using something other than my own gifts and talents to keep me moving forward—or I'd not have been so struck by seeing the prosthetic limbs. Perhaps I rely too heavily on enjoying the success of others so that I don't strive as hard as I can to achieve my own goals. On the other hand, it could be a reminder to be grateful that I am walking on my own limbs. These two interpretations appear contradictory, though both can be true. As

I mentioned earlier, grappling with paradox is one of the challenges of seeing things metaphorically. I had "ahas" from all of the possible interpretations. Seeing these men reminded me that I am walking my chosen path, and though the way is long and sometimes seems pointless, it is following the path that matters.

Whether or not the Universe, or God, or the Collective Unconscious put these men in my path just so I would notice them is not the point. At least, not to me. What matters is that I chose to see the symbolism in the moment and used it to try to understand myself more deeply, to become more conscious of my own behaviors and patterns so that I can move toward a healthier response to the world.

Visitors' Rights and Responsibilities

When traveling to the Invisible Realm, there are certain rights and responsibilities that apply, just as they do when we travel in the waking world. When I visit the Invisible Realm, I have the right to my own experience, and to the interpretation of that experience. I can ask for assistance from other travelers, whether they be intuitives or dream readers or friends, but ultimately what I learn from the Invisible Realm is my own experience. So I have the right to believe in my own experience. I've had many moments in my life that clearly demonstrate to me the reality of psychic connection involving empathy, intuition, and telepathy. I have no need to prove the reality of those phenomena to anyone else, because I know from my own experience that they exist.

With the right to believe my own experience, though, comes the responsibility to allow others to have and believe in their own experiences. Having been raised by skeptical parents, my "rational" mind usually questions the possibility that someone (even myself) has experienced something science can't (yet) explain. But that doesn't give me the right to belittle or negate someone else's personal experience. My main responsibility is to respect other travelers' tales and to learn from them what I can. Keeping an open mind is essential.

In addition to the right to believe my own experience, I have the responsibility not to take anyone else's word for what is truth. I may listen carefully to teachers, and try their methods for gaining wisdom, but the two touchstones of truth for me are whether I have an "aha," or whether I experience something for myself. Remember the story of the Taylormade sign? That was when I finally understood in my marrow Jeremy Taylor's statement, "I know this is true, and it's much too important to take my word for it."

The only way we can say what is true is to examine what we're taught and measure that against the understanding we've gained from our own experiences. If everyone would examine what their teachers tell them, really dig into the information and hold it close, look at it from different points of view, and *then* decide whether that information has the ring of truth to it, the world would be safer. We'd have fewer zealots who hang their passionate quest for meaning onto the first convenient guru and then do whatever that guru tells them to do.

There is also a responsibility to use the information I receive from the Invisible Realm for my own growing consciousness, which enables the growth of collective consciousness, rather than for any manipulative gain. The power of positive thinking is an excellent practice for seeing the bright side of life and creating the belief in myself that I deserve to be treated well and that the Universe will support me in a path of learning. If I use information to hurt or swindle others, though, I've removed myself from the possibility of any true gain.

What to Bring

Ready to pack your bag? The best part of traveling in the Invisible Realm is that there's no need to remember your toothbrush, towel, or change of clothes. The main thing to bring is your curiosity—that desire to discover new information about yourself, and the world.

You might also want to bring a journal, and write down your dreams, waking life synchronicities, questions, and insights. This traveler's diary will help you find your way.

No need to worry about bringing your imagination, because your imagination is the vessel that carries you there. Trust it to navigate the currents and ride the waves.

Part Two:

Accessing the Invisible Realm

Imagination and Curiosity

Visiting the Invisible Realm gets easier with practice, and all practicing takes is focused attention. Let's start with imagination.

When someone tells us a story, if we're paying attention, our imaginations will create a personal version of the story. Whether it's someone's dream, the report of a near-miss in traffic, or an oft-heard complaint like "My co-worker is driving me crazy," I will imagine these scenes or scenarios for myself, and bring along all of my associations. As humans, we are imagining stories, plans, religion, art, and explanations for things all the time.

For instance, let me tell you a story. One of my college jobs was indexing government documents at the library. The man who trained me told me one of the brochures was about the problem of lead buckshot being consumed by wildlife, which then sickened and died from lead poisoning. The title of the pamphlet was "Save Our Wildlife: Use Steel Buckshot." The irony delighted me, and made me wonder if the author had been aware of the humor. I told the story to my brother, who also got a good laugh out of it.

Three or four years later, my brother and I lived in different and distant states and had for most of the intervening time. We wrote letters from time to time, and the story of the pamphlet title came up once. I'd been thinking of it for some reason, and reminded him of it in a letter. A couple of days after I sent it, I received one from him, dated the same day as mine. In it he asked, "What was that story about the steel buckshot?"

Make of the coincidence what you will, but if you were engaged in the story as you read it, you imagined it for yourself. Take a moment to picture what came up when I told you the job was in a library. Did you see a generic stack of books? A library you frequent now? Or saw once? Or some abstract library created in your imagination with bits and pieces of memories of a lot of libraries? Some readers may protest that they didn't imagine any of those things, but just understood the concept of "library" from the word itself.

Whatever your experience, welcome to the Invisible Realm! We met in that imagined space, across the time of my writing the story to the time of your reading it. I imagine you imagining my story as I tell it, and now you can imagine me doing that. What complex structures we build with our imaginations! All with the telling of a story.

This is one of the easiest ways to access the Invisible Realm. Next time someone tells you a story, pay attention to the images that arise. Maybe the story makes you feel something. Maybe it makes you think of a story of your own. All of these associations are information we access from the Invisible Realm. Finding the reasons behind the associations leads to insight and greater self-understanding.

Imagination and curiosity are what lead to innovation, scientific discoveries, art, conscious living, and a whole host of other good things. The shadow side of it is that we have, as humans, this painfully sharp talent for imagining horrible things to do to one another, ourselves, and the world. It's interesting that we can apply our focused intention and attention on creating new kinds of destruction, and yet remain unaware of the urgings that prompt us to desire that destruction in the first place. When we become conscious of our underlying motivations, we can shift our energies to creative endeavors instead.

Our imaginations are so eager to serve us that sometimes it doesn't even take focused attention to get them to play. For instance, we sometimes notice patterns in the grain of a wood panel or in a cloud. The fact that I project some association onto an inanimate object or cloud patterns tells me something metaphorical about myself. It provides information for my psyche to play with, for my intuition to help me understand. The more I notice the patterns, and the more I ask myself why I see that particular pattern, the more I grow toward conscious relationship with the world.

A skeptic might argue that the images we project onto the clouds (or ink blots, or patterns on wood paneling) are meaningless, because our minds are programmed to look for patterns as a survival skill, and so we see patterns where we don't need to. This is certainly one way to view the phenomenon, but if we agree that our brains are hard-wired to seek patterns in the chaos, it seems to me an act of great hubris to dismiss the patterns we do see as meaningless. Why assume that because we can't understand the message, there is no message there?

If the Universe, or my unconscious, sends me a message, and the Universe has programmed my brain to look for patterns, I want to try to understand that message. For me, when I consider what I see as a metaphor, I often have an "aha" moment. Sometimes the "aha" feels quieter, or smaller, then what I experience with dream reading, but never insignificant. If I see a dragon in the cloud, I might think of the metaphor that we all have dragons of impulse, which urge us to this behavior or that, and the one that will win is the one we feed. Which reminds me of the expression, "Where attention goes, energy flows," encouraging me to examine my thoughts and actions to make sure I'm feeding the dragons that I want to grow.

Dreams and Projection

Working with Your Dreams

The first step in working with your dreams is to record them in as much detail as you can remember. "I see I've left the lights on in the cabin" is good, but, "I see I've left *two* lights on in the *wooden* cabin" is even better. Each of the small details, "two" and "wooden," provide valuable clues to the meanings of the dream. Working off of common experience, "two" suggests the duality by which new ideas arise into consciousness, so whatever the message of the dream is, it's a new realization. "Wood" is a great example of the wisdom of looking at homonyms and Klang associations (words that have similar, but not exactly the same sound) in dreams. In American English, "wood" and "would" sound the same. And, as it turns out, when something is identified as being made of wood in a dream, dreamers report a lot of "aha" moments when they consider the dream in terms of desires of the spirit: "What would I do if I could do anything?" Or, "What would I do if I knew I couldn't fail?" Is there some sense of what I (maybe secretly) want to do that the other symbols in the dream speak to? (Interestingly, Jeremy Taylor reports that the association between "wood" and "would" holds true in Korean, which doesn't have the homonym relationship.)

What if you don't remember your dreams? Pay attention to the subtle clues when you wake: Is there a lingering emotion? A song or phrase stuck in your head? Does your mind immediately go to a certain memory, one that seems random in the context of your waking life? All of these things can be clues to the messages your dreams were trying to provide. Science has shown that everyone dreams, though not everyone remembers those dreams. But you know that sometimes people wake up in a bad mood or "On the wrong side of the bed." When dreams want to get our attention, they will linger into waking life, one way or another.

It all comes back to paying attention. By noticing, sketching, or writing down these subtle signals, my psyche gets the message that I, the dreamer, am interested in this. And though it may take some practice, paying attention to the small things leads to better dream recall over time. And if all else fails, sign up for a dream reading workshop or session. It often happens that a person will have much improved dream recall just prior to such an event. And if even that fails, try making up a dream. Make it as absurd or mundane as you like, maybe even a collage of random waking life memories. Whatever comes out of these endeavors can be read metaphorically, as you would read a dream.

In the beginning, when you hear a dream (or review one of your own), consider what general impressions you have about the dream. Then consider the symbols specifically mentioned in a dream. In a long, detailed dream, start with the symbols that most interest you. What associations do you have with the individual symbol? If you consider the symbols in pairs, what new associations arise? This may seem challenging at first, but when your psyche is confronted with the question, it will try to answer.

You can also notice places where you wrote the wrong word in recording your dream. For example, "tiles" is written as "titles" or "tilts." How does this new word inform the dream? If the tiles are symbols of titles, what does that suggest to you? Or does the whole dream "tilt" on this place in the dream?

Beyond that, it just takes practice, and trusting your intuition. It is, however, much easier to see the metaphorical meaning in other people's dreams than in one's own. Our dreams come to lead us to greater understanding, and our conscious mind is generally content with having figured out everything thus far, so that the next new thing is often just beyond our grasp. This is why working dreams in groups is such a wonderful process. The original dreamer receives insights from others, and those reading their own meanings into their imagined versions of the dreams learn about themselves in the process.

The Idea of Projection

As I mentioned earlier, when listening to stories, we imagine the story for ourselves. So too with dreams. This imagining, just like seeing shapes in clouds, is projection. So when we talk about other people's dreams, the only thing we can talk about with any authority is what we imagine for ourselves when hearing the dream. It's a good idea, when talking about dreams, to stay aware of this projection and own the insights for ourselves. The simplest way to do this is to use the technique pioneered by Montague Ullman and popularized by teachers like Jeremy Taylor and Robert Moss. That is, to frame all statements about the dream in the first person, including such phrases as "When I imagine this dream," or "In my imagined version of the dream." This makes clear the fact that the statement is a projection, and makes it much safer for the original dreamer to hear what's being said. If the comment is in the second person, there's a certain accusatory tone, "Your dream shows that you had a big problem with your father," is much less likely to trigger an "aha" than, "When I imagine this dream, I am reminded that I had a big problem with my father." The original dreamer has the mental breathing space to consider whether the statement might be true for him, without getting defensive about the idea, because the speaker has owned this for herself.

But what if the speaker didn't have such a problem with her father? Does this invalidate what she has to say? The beauty of the "When I imagine this dream for myself," format is that the speaker must first imagine the problem in order to even consciously form a projection upon it. Whatever the speaker imagines is her own construct, her own understanding of how the world works. It is at these levels that she owns her projections onto the dream. I've often heard Jeremy Taylor model this in his workshops, prefacing his comments with something like, "When I imagine myself as a young woman just graduating from college...." Using this structure within the language serves as a reminder that all I can comment on about another person's dream is the version I imagine for myself.

The fact that the speaker's response is constructed in her own imagination doesn't necessarily invalidate the accuracy of her projections. And sometimes just the opposite is true. If, when I hear a dream, I don't have a strong "aha" association, my imagining of the symbols might rely at first on theory, which is the collection of archetypal meanings that elicit "aha" moments most reliably. I've learned these meanings from working with dreams in groups. I've never heard a dream, for instance, where death does not represent, at one level, profound transformation and change. Again, this wouldn't be the first thing that arose for me if it weren't true for me, and when I dream of death, it's a meaning I always consider. Offering these archetypal meanings to the dreamer, who may not be consciously aware of them, can awaken profound understanding.

I may also have some idiosyncratic associations that arise when I hold the symbol in my imagination. These too can bring deeper understanding to the dream, even though I, as the one imagining the dream, can't see what the connection might be. For example, I heard a dream which featured Acapulco as a location. We had discussed the dream for quite some time, but no one had brought up the location as a symbol. My only association with Acapulco is from a family vacation when I was eleven years old. My older brother and sister played in waves which were too alarming for me, and ended up with badly skinned knees. When this memory came to mind as I listen to the dream, I dismissed it as too personal and couldn't imagine what it might have to do with the dream. As the group took turns offering their projections, this memory arose twice more, at which point I knew I needed to bring it into the circle. I explained to the dreamer that I wasn't sure how it might apply, but shared the memory with her. Her eyes widened in surprise, which is often a signal for an "aha." She associated Acapulco with a certain romantic relationship, and my memory of the rough waves I'd seen there gave her further insight into the meanings of her dream.

The Dream Work Tool Kit

Jeremy Taylor has a wealth of knowledge about working with dreams in groups, and summed up what he found to be the essential points in his Dream Work Tool Kit, included here with his permission.

The Dream Work Tool Kit: Six Basic Hints for Dream Work

One

All dreams speak a universal language and come in the service of health and wholeness. There is no such thing as a "bad dream"—only dreams that sometimes take a dramatically negative form in order to grab our attention.

Two

Only the dreamer can say with any certainty what meanings his or her dream may have. This certainty usually comes in the form of a wordless "aha!" of recognition. This "aha" is a function of memory, and is the only reliable touchstone of dream work.

Three

There is no such thing as a dream with only one meaning. All dreams and dream images are "overdetermined," and have multiple meanings and layers of significance.

Four

No dreams come just to tell you what you already know. All dreams break new ground and invite you to new understandings and insights.

Five

When talking to others about their dreams, it is both wise and polite to preface your remarks with words to the effect of "in my imagined version of the dream...," and to keep this commentary in the first person as much as possible. This means that even relatively challenging comments can be made in such a way that the dreamer may actually be able to hear and internalize them. It also can become a profound psycho-spiritual discipline—"walking a mile in your neighbor's moccasins."

Six

All dream group participants should agree at the outset to maintain anonymity in all discussions of dream work. In the absence of any specific request for confidentiality, group members should be free to discuss their experiences openly outside the group, provided no other dreamer is identifiable in their stories. However, whenever any group member requests confidentiality, all members should agree to be bound automatically by such a request.

© *Jeremy Taylor 2005*

I first encountered Jeremy's Tool Kit in 2000 when I attended his workshop at Naropa University. The feeling that I knew him haunted me as I listened to his introductory talk on Friday evening, though I knew we hadn't met. When I introduced myself after the talk, he asked, "Have we met?" I looked familiar to him as well. I'd had this happen before, with people I was meeting for the first time. Each of them had turned out to be important to me as my life unfolded. Any lingering doubt I had about spending the money for the full weekend workshop vanished.

At the workshop, my name was pulled from the hat, selecting me to share a dream. The dream featured a combine tractor and evergreen boughs and the work quickly touched on important themes in my life, eliciting strong "aha" moments, and even a moment of vehement protest, which Jeremy had warned was also an "aha," or the strength of protest wouldn't be necessary to protect long-held beliefs about myself. By the final session on Sunday morning, I'd had the space to understand the reaction and accept it. That morning I learned that when I acknowledge a blind spot to Jeremy, he always meets it with gentle humor and understanding, because of the compassion he's developed from years of dream work.

In the years since, I've read dreams using the Tool Kit as my guide. I've come to understand for myself how deeply this work connects people, fostering compassion and understanding in large groups and small ones. We build sacred trust with one another as we journey together into deeper self-understanding. Profound healing occurs as we are "seen" by others through the lens of the dream. The language of metaphor helps us speak truths that touch us in places words don't usually reach, and helps us heal in unexpected ways.

After my mom died, I thought I was holding it together pretty well. Following on the heels of the initial sense of unreality, I pulled myself together for a reunion of my husband's side of the family, and jumped into the preparations for Mom's memorial service. All the activity left little room for grieving. Three days after the service, I developed bronchitis, and a few days after that, I sat in a dream circle, my psyche shattered with grief. I met with Jeremy for breakfast and complained that it felt like my sister was getting all the signs from the universe that Mom was sending. Jeremy handled it in his usual gentle way, probing a bit to see if I'd felt less loved than my sister, to which I could honestly say no. I admitted to feeling sorry for myself nonetheless.

And then that afternoon, my name came out of the hat. I had a feeling beforehand that I didn't really want to work the dream I'd been thinking of, and I paged through my journal at break and found two squirrel dreams. So I worked those. With the mother squirrel in one dream leaving her baby as a gift before departing the building, I received a lot of projections about my mom, including her habit of "squirreling things away," and about the sense of being marked, since one of the squirrels had peed on me in the dream. At the end of the hour or so, I sat drained but immensely grateful to have been the focus of the loving attention of the circle of dreamers. Afterward, I told two of the dreamers that I felt like I'd come in and dropped the shattered parts of myself in the center of the circle like a pile of pickup sticks, and the group had gathered those together into a tidy bundle and given them back to me.

In the morning, I repeated the comment to the entire group to express my gratitude, and Jeremy told us about how he'd gotten in a car after that bit of dream work and it smelled faintly of squirrel. He inquired, and the driver said he traps nuisance squirrels in the city and takes them out into the countryside for release, and had just done that before coming to get Jeremy. In the circle, Jeremy used this story as an illustration of the continued invitation to trust the "aha" moments I'd had in the dream work.

At this level of trust, I've gone beyond faith, though faith is still a part of what I feel. I've come to *know* that this work of reading dreams helps me live in greater understanding of what I am called to do in this life. I live in deeper compassion with other people, having come to the knowledge that at root, we humans suffer similar wounds and search for the answers to similar questions. And having witnessed, over and over again, how several people in a dream group will get physical tingles from the insights offered, I've come to see that there are truths we share, just by living on this earth together.

I remember a couple of conversations with my daughter when she was younger. She'd been thinking a lot about the evolution of life on the planet. Ideas suggested in science class started her imagining the long evolutionary history of species, the interrelatedness of species, and the origins of life itself. Heady stuff, trying to hold millennia upon millennia in our thoughts. When I think about the questions she brought up, it takes me to the Mystery beyond the mystery. That realm of understanding beyond an incarnated human's. Possibly beyond the disincarnate soul's perceptions as well. The reason behind life itself, the true Creator, or if there is no Creator, the great Nothing from which Everything spontaneously arose—all of these lie within the mystery of the divine. We humans get glimpses of the mystery, or glimpses of reflections of the mystery, in our dreams. Sometimes we have a pure experience of the Divine, as I did in the dream I had in my mid-twenties:

I walk into a cave and find a corpse. Its decomposition horrifies me, and I turn to run. And then I think, "I'm supposed to turn and face my fears." And when I turn around, the corpse is gone. In its place, there towers a blindingly white, radiant angel. He tells me he loves me, and he couldn't be with me in this life, but he is always with me. I woke from this dream overcome with emotion. Joy, grief, and wonder were all equally present, equally true. Time and time again in my life I've found comfort in the memory of that dream.

Even in the reading of quieter dreams, the Invisible Realm makes itself known. Every dream worker I know responds to dreams at some level or another from intuition. In my experience, when someone truly trusts the ideas that spring forth, even those seemingly unconnected to the dream, these insights prove to touch closest to home for the original dreamer and for the group as a whole. It requires attention, both to the dream and to the intuitive nudges that arise upon hearing it. With some practice, intuition about the meanings of dreams grows stronger.

The more you work with dreams, the more you'll notice trends and themes. One of the basic themes is that dreams come to show us what we don't already consciously know. The things we don't consciously know are often referred to as "shadow." Collectively and individually, we carry around a lot of shadow. When we project onto others, we see in them qualities or behaviors that we are unwilling or unable to see in ourselves. These projections include the shadow behaviors considered dark: everything from dishonesty to inhumanity. The twentieth century offered us example after example of genocide and war, fierce and unrelenting expressions of dark shadow energy. This may show up in dreams as nightmare figures: thugs, murderers, or rapists. When we have dreams like this, we often wake in a cold sweat with a pounding heart, the dream image unforgettable. These dreams are especially helpful to read in a group, as they transform from terrifying to enlightening. They are helpful in allowing us to see where our own prejudices lie, so that we can stay aware when they arise in waking life.

But there's also a bright shadow, in which we find it easier to see talents and abilities in others before we see it in ourselves. When exceptionally bright, charismatic, talented people arrive in our dreams, it helps to remember that everything and everyone in the dream is some symbolic representation of the dreamer. That means that the talented, brilliant, loving people in our dreams are parts of ourselves that we may not fully own yet. Dreams can help us see our own gifts and abilities in this way.

Lucid Dreaming

When a dreamer becomes aware in a dream that he is dreaming, we say he's "lucid." Traditionally, the definition of lucid dreaming is that the dreamer forms the thought "This is a dream," or "I'm dreaming." When this happens to me, I may attempt to control the direction of the dream, and indeed it may appear that my dream ego is taking over and making things happen. Unless what I "want" to happen in the dream is in accordance with what the dream has come to teach me, my efforts will generally be answered in ways I didn't anticipate. One example from my own dreams might illustrate this. *In the dream, I am walking with an old man. As we walk, I realize I'm dreaming, and decide to ask him for answers about the big questions in my life at the time—"Am I on the right career path? What does the future hold if I keep on in this direction?" The man points to a woman who is walking ahead of us and says, "She knows." I get very excited that I'm close to the answer I seek, and then the woman turns around and I realize that it's me.*

In this dream, my lucidity prompted my dream ego to ask the question most on my mind in waking life at the time of the dream. I'd given years to developing my craft as a novelist, and had spent years studying dreams, and neither one seemed to be bringing me any closer to an actual career that I could rely on for income. Yet the dream chose not to answer the question directly, with a promise of future success or the advice to give it all up and find a "real" job, one where I'd earn wages. Instead, the dream shows me that in my heart, I do know what I'm supposed to be doing with my life, and that I should trust myself.

While some people report that they are able to direct the action in their dreams at will, even these dreams carry multiple layers of meaning that can be discovered through dream reading. The "hidden" layers of meaning will likely create very strong "aha" moments for the original dreamer, as the unconscious finds ways to get its message across in even the most lucid and scripted dreams. For example, one of the most common responses to becoming lucid in a dream is to fly. Whether the flying resembles that of a bird or is just floating off the ground or some other configuration, the sense of defying gravity is what the dreamer seeks. I've learned that, for me and many others, this is because flying in dreams is often a symbol for the desire for more creative expression.

If we are, indeed, created in "God's image," my understanding is that the way in which we are most like the divine energy that permeates the universe is in our urge to create. We, as humans, are innately creative. It's what has enabled everything from soaring musical compositions to the technological domination of the planet. Yet many of us subsume our creative energies because they don't fit neatly into our 9 to 5 lives, and if we do, our dreams will come to urge us to find ways to express ourselves. Flying in dreams is both a reminder that the urge is there and a celebration of any recent waking life attempts to give that creative urge a voice. Flying is also the ability to defy gravity, which is one of the laws of the physical world that we all must live with. In that sense, flying is about escaping from conventional rules about how to live.

In *The Wisdom of Your Dreams*, Jeremy Taylor proposes that the traditional understanding of lucidity in a dream is insufficient. There are dreams in which the dreamer realizes something about the situation that is surprising, like, "I'm breathing under water," and the dreamer understands that the act doesn't fit with her usual experience.[3] Even without the words "Oh, this is a dream," the dreamer may experience the realization that the world is behaving strangely and that there is metaphorical resonance with this odd behavior. Or the dreamer may have a dream and then in the next dream, tell someone about the first dream, as a dream. The dreamer understands that the previous experience was a dream, even though she hasn't woken up between them.

The most useful aspect of lucid dreaming is the ability to address problems in waking life that may be deeply entrenched. If the dreamer can become lucid while being pursued and remember to turn and face his pursuer, he will generally reach profound depths of understanding and healing around the problem. Asking other dream characters, whether pursuers or bystanders, or even inanimate objects, what their purpose in the dream is, can generate interesting answers that lead to new insights.

---

[3] Taylor, *The Wisdom of Your Dreams*, pp. 253-256.

Recurring Dreams

When dreams return over and over, or when dream themes recur even if the "story" around the theme changes, these are telling the dreamer that something essential is at stake. Having an idea of when the dreams started and stopped in life—was it a phenomenon of my childhood that I dreamed over and over of being pursued by a man with knife, or did the recurring dreams start in my adulthood?— can help the dreamer understand what the core meaning of the dream is. In the example I gave, a man with a knife represents to me my fear of embracing my own masculine (because the dream figure is a man) intellectual power (because the knife represents intellect). The dream haunted me most in my childhood, but has recurred more sporadically through adulthood. I can honestly say that this is a struggle I've engaged in since my childhood, when being "smart" in school was not a way to find social acceptance. The patterns of behavior I developed in childhood in order to deal with the need to fit in (hiding my intelligence rather than owning it) might have helped me survive emotionally in the classroom, but were not serving me on a soul level. Those patterns we develop as children to navigate our lives often end up thwarting us in adulthood, as they generally involve compartmentalizing or shutting off various parts of ourselves, and we need to have access to those parts in order to be whole human beings.

A recurring dream that begins in adulthood will often point to a recurring situation in waking life that the dreamer isn't addressing with full consciousness, and so isn't responding to in the best way possible. These dreams might refer to workplace dramas, or relationship problems, or parenting challenges. They might point to childhood issues that were so suppressed the dreamer has no recall of dreaming about them as a child or even that they occurred in waking life. Physical, sexual, and emotional abuse are often traumatic enough that memory of them is suppressed or avoided until such time that the dreamer is emotionally able to confront the memories and bring about healing.

Paradox and Conflicting Memories of Dream Events

Dream symbols carry multiple associations, and quite frequently, people in a dream circle offering their projections on a dream will come up with apparently contradictory interpretations of a symbol. Yet the dreamer may have "aha" responses to both of these projections. Using the example from above, flying in dreams can be both a celebration of recent creative expression and a nudge to really let that creativity flow. Our rationalist minds want to say, "Which is it? Either I'm being patted on the back for doing a good job or being told I need to do a better job." Both of these can be true. In fact, if one pursues dream reading far enough, paradoxes inevitably arise. Such a paradox in waking life might be that my soul needs to both nurture my children as deeply and carefully as I am capable, and I also need to have time away from nurturing my children, leaving them in someone else's care, in order to engage with my creative longings. I can't possibly be present for my children as much as my mothering instinct demands and still remain faithful to the inspirations that demand time and attention.

Another example that comes to mind is that of a dreamer I know who saw her mother's stunted creative expression and vowed to not follow that example. By embracing her own creativity, the dreamer, in a sense, betrays her mother, who was unable to do the same. But *not* embracing her creativity would also be a betrayal of her mother, who wanted only the best for her daughter's life and sacrificed her own creativity in order that her daughter could live a creative life. The point of the paradox is an uncomfortable place to be, and the best solution is for the dreamer to become consciously aware of the choices she's making. When bridges show up in dreams, they are often pointing to the successful navigation of such a paradox in the dreamer's waking life.

In a similar way, dreams may present scenarios that appear paradoxical. For example, I might dream that I'm in a car, yet I remember both that I was driving the car and that I was sitting in the passenger seat with someone else driving the car. Such dream reports are often interpreted as incomplete recall or confusion as our rational, waking minds remind us that it must be one or the other. In fact, the dream can do whatever it wants, and it chooses to show me both in the driver's seat and in the passenger seat with someone else at the wheel. This ability to hold two view points in the dream is also sometimes expressed as being both a participant in the dream action and a removed observer. Jeremy Taylor suggests that such instances point to a growing compassion—the ability to see things from more than one point of view.[4] It's always valuable to read the dream in its entirety, so the dreamer can understand, for instance, what it means that she's both the driver and passenger in a situation.

Anxiety Dreams

Many people experience dreams in which they can't find a classroom, or have to take a test they didn't even know about, or are about to go on stage and don't know what the play is, much less their lines. Such dreams are generally accompanied by a lot of anxiety, and the mood can linger after waking. These types of dreams can verge on nightmares, though the danger is not to the dreamer's imagined body, as it would be with a monster chasing him, but rather to his reputation. The risk is failure, humiliation, and embarrassment. The carefully constructed public persona that the dreamer shows the world is in danger of collapsing. Whether the dreamer needs to remember that there are life lessons to attend to (school dreams), or spiritual work that needs attention (job dreams), or a situation in which the dreamer needs to be ready even without feeling ready (theater), these dreams invite the dreamer to look at the spiritual school/work/performance that he may be neglecting.

---

[4] Taylor, *The Wisdom of Your Dreams,* pp. 263-264.

Nightmares

If you've read this far, I hope you've begun to see that all dreams can be read metaphorically. This is especially important to remember when thinking about nightmares. Dreams that frighten or terrify us into wakefulness are impossible to ignore, and their meanings are important to explore. Often, when dreamers allow others to hold in conscious awareness the thing that frightens them most, and reflect back other understandings, profound blessings of insight arise. I've seen the most terrifying dreams give birth to the deepest healing.

When unconscious messages really want to get our attention, they often appear couched in a nightmare form, precisely so we don't forget them. When I wake in heart-pounding terror, I will remember the content of the dream, or at least, certainly, the final image. Whether I see the death of a loved one or an intruder is trying to get into my house or I'm facing a monster, the dream images bring a wealth of information about something urgent in my life. It might be a physical health warning, or it might be a deeply significant spiritual yearning that I've been ignoring, but the dream will have a message that, if I ignore it, will only come back again in another dream. The unconscious is persistent.

Even the recurring nightmares that often accompany post-traumatic stress disorder can respond to the focus of conscious awareness. Lucid dreaming can facilitate healing. Robert Waggoner, who has studied lucid dreaming extensively, states, "By most accounts, the psychological tool of lucid dreaming has led to successful outcomes. Normally after the PTSD sufferer becomes lucidly aware just once in the nightmare scenario, the nightmares virtually cease. In some cases the PTSD sufferer shows positive benefits from simply hearing about the idea of lucid dreaming."[5]

Lucidity isn't necessary, though, to understand and work with most nightmares. Since most people can't forget a nightmare even if they want to, recording them is generally easier than remembering other dreams. If you remember a nightmare from any time in your life, exploring the symbols within it will open the door to greater understanding.

Poetry

Like dreams, poems speak soul to soul. When people are touched by poems, the experience is the same as a dream reading "aha." The emotion of a poem and the exquisite expression of the personal so that it becomes universal, touch the receiver of a poem through metaphor. In those moments of understanding, there lies healing. Kim Rosen, an advocate for learning poems by heart, says,

---

[5] Robert Waggoner, Psychological Healing Through Lucid Dreaming," *Dream Time*, Spring 2013, p. 13.

"Poetry can be a lantern that shines into dark places within us. Poems can be powerful medicine for personal transformation."[6]

The best way to find poetry that speaks to your soul is to read widely at first, and then pursue the work of the poets you like best. Read the poems aloud. Or get on video sharing sites and search for spoken word poetry. I've experienced a lot of amazing work in the comfort of my home. In particular, I was captivated by Andrea Gibson, and then Sarah Kay and Phil Kaye. Spoken word poetry and written poetry enter our awareness in different ways, yet both rely on the language of metaphor, just like dreams. They're so much alike that those of us who think about dreams and poems a lot often inadvertently interchange the words. These slips of the tongue invite us to see the metaphorical relationship between dreams and poems.

I recommend committing a poem to memory. I begin by reading it several times a day, holding the sequence of images in my mind as best I can. After a number of readings, when I feel like I'm getting the hang of it, I test myself, checking the printed copy as necessary. The repetition becomes a kind of rosary; one that speaks to my soul, because I have chosen, or even written the poem. The words carry a cadence I can feel in my voice and chest, a vibration that I also sense just beyond the physical boundary of my body. I take the poem into myself, make it even more my own by using it as a prayer. Then, when I say it aloud for others, it comes from a sacred

---

[6] Alison Luterman, "Written on the Bones: Kim Rosen on Reclaiming the Ancient Power of Poetry," *The Sun Magazine*, December 2010, p. 5.

place and offers the chance for our souls to touch and share an understanding of ourselves and our world.

Music often moves us deeply as well, with or without words. Diana Deutsch, Professor of Psychology at the University of California, San Diego, studies the connection between speech and singing. You can hear about her work on Radiolab.[7] She discovered that a snippet of speech on an endless loop switches from spoken to sung in the listener's perception of it. She also studied perfect pitch and found it much higher among music students who grew up with a tonal language, such as Mandarin or Vietnamese, than those who grew up speaking English. The same show discusses how our brains are wired to find patterns in sounds, which is why the chaotic pulsing of dissonance irritates us, while consonance—a beautiful chord— relaxes and calms us.[8]

Understanding these phenomena from a purely physical perspective is fascinating, but doesn't negate that humans have strong emotional and physical reactions to poetry and music. Prayer is often embodied in poetry and music, such as the Psalms of the Bible. The individual experience of a poem will vary from person to person, and even from one repetition to another. Yet because we are, in many fundamental ways, alike as human beings, there's general consistency between audience response to the work: a moving tragedy elicits a far different response than a clever comedy. In that shared response to a poem, or a dream, or any work of art, we find a

---

[7] http://www.radiolab.org/2007/sep/24/behaves-so-strangely/

[8] http://www.radiolab.org/2007/sep/24/sound-as-touch/

community of like-minded people. Anything that can bring us to greater understanding of one another is worth spending time on, so I urge you to sing, or read a poem, or play your favorite music. The Invisible Realm is that close.

Prayer and Meditation

Many people connect to the Invisible Realm through prayer and meditation. In my experience, prayer is the focused attention on and even an attempt at attunement with the Divine. Prayer is meditation in which I offer my heartfelt gratitude and hopes to the Creative Energy of the Universe. I pray for the wellbeing of other people, as well as for the assistance I need to navigate the challenges of life. But even more importantly, I offer thanks for the beauty and blessings I see in the world. I hear Jeremy Taylor's voice quoting Meister Eckhart: "If the only prayer you ever say is thank you, that will be enough." Focusing on life's blessings lightens the burdens.

Meditation is more challenging for me. I can follow a guided meditation fairly easily, and have found that certain images (grounding, letting divine light enter through the top of my head, etc.) are extremely helpful in calming my emotions and creating a sense of peace. However, thoughts still distract me when I attempt Zen meditation. Others, however, are more successful at letting those distractions go. And whether you're meditating on your breath or on some more complicated visualization, meditation leads into the Invisible Realm.

Oracles

When we consult oracles, we project our own imagination on what is seen or heard. Traditionally, oracles were people through whom gods and goddesses spoke. The word has grown to include methods of accessing wisdom that can be found in the Invisible Realm, including the Tarot, the I Ching, and other methods. What matters most is what we bring to the consultation of oracles. For example, the same tarot card in two different readings might have profoundly different meanings for the querent (the person asking the question), or a card in a reading will elicit varying "ahas" from the reader and the querent, even if both are familiar with the archetypes and usual associations or interpretations of the card. The beauty of projection and our built-in need for finding patterns of meaning in the world around us is that anything in our waking world can act as a mirror for us to gaze into. Oracles are a way to focus the mind and offer it a mirror to consider. As the questioner gazes into the ball or at the image on the card, the question of relationship between what I see and my question for the universe invites my brain to find connections, and in those connections I often find the "aha" of insight.

Do oracles tell the future? For some people, I'm sure that they do. Just as some people are gifted with a lot of precognitive dreams, some tap into that intuitive knowledge pathway through oracles and find them a reliable source of information about what's to come. Others find the guidance in the I Ching never steers them wrong, or that a certain card always turns up when a certain problem is present in their lives.

But if you don't yet have that relationship with oracles, how can you use them effectively? Practice is certainly part of it. Experimentation and curiosity, and noticing patterns, will all help you find your own way. Try several oracles to discover which speaks most clearly to your imagination. If possible, play around with each of the oracles discussed below.

Over the course of history, people have turned to everything from tea leaves to pools of water in the attempt to read messages from the Invisible Realm. My purpose in this book isn't to cover every oracle I've ever heard of, but rather to discuss the ones I'm more familiar with in order to convey a sense of how to work with oracles. It's my experience that any oracle may offer insight to the seeker because the seeker projects consciously and unconsciously onto it, and many people have found that after working with a particular oracle for a while, synchronicities that are mysterious and satisfying occur with increasing frequency. It's up to the seeker to determine and assign meanings to what's seen and whatever synchronicities occur.

Tarot

"The Tarot is a symbolic map of consciousness and an ancient book of wisdom that reveals to us visually and symbolically the creative ideas and states of consciousness that appear in multiple existence in all cultures. The seventy-eight symbols are portraitures and archetypes of inner and outer experiences that are prevalent within human experience."[9]

From the time I was two, when Santa got a little confused and put the weaponry-themed deck of cards in my stocking and the flower-backed deck in my brother's, I've been fascinated by playing cards. It took years and years for my brother and me to realize that the decks we had were likely meant for the other, and by that time, we'd used the decks so much it didn't occur to us to trade. In childhood, I mostly played Solitaire or built houses with my cards, but then when I was eleven years old my family traveled to Mexico and I discovered that not every culture used the same deck of cards. Instead of diamonds, there were coins. For hearts, there were cups. The spades were swords and the clubs were, well, big wooden clubs. In the deck I bought, they look a little more like gourds. And the tens aren't just tens, but are extra court cards.

----

[9] Arrien, *The Tarot Handbook*, p. 12.

I was hooked. From then on, wherever I traveled, I sought out decks of cards for souvenirs. Less intentionally, I gathered more decks as birthday gifts, or "free with seven box tops" sort of prizes. And at some point in my teens, I discovered tarot decks, which bore a much stronger resemblance to my cards from Mexico than they did to the cards of my childhood. But even better, they came with a whole extra set of cards in addition to the Ace through King I was used to. The ones that had become playing cards were the Minor Arcana. The cards in the Major Arcana, I learned, represented archetypal concepts. The best thing about tarot decks, in my mind, was that every single card bore an image, often elaborately and gorgeously illustrated.

The images awakened my imagination, as did the traditional meanings of each card. Always curious about what my future would hold, I turned to the Tarot with my questions. Early on, I sought prediction in the readings. I wanted to know exactly what would happen. I found myself disappointed that the cards didn't reveal things more clearly and accurately.

Now that I've immersed myself for so long in metaphor, I've come to use the readings as a way to catch glimpses of possible futures, but with the understanding that I'm projecting meaning onto the spread and it may or may not tell me what the future holds. Sometimes a single card will keep showing up over the course of weeks of readings and then I won't pull it again for months or years. I pay attention to those patterns, of course, and I've come to trust that those patterns hold meaning.

When I use a tarot deck for a reading, I shuffle the deck six times (that being my lucky number) and then either cut the deck and deal out the pattern of the reading, or spread the deck out on the table and then hold my hand over the deck and slowly move it over all the cards. I often get a sudden warmth or coolness over one part of the deck, and I select the card under my hand at that point. This is a way of practicing the awareness of subtle energies as well as a way to choose a card.

The Tarot is also a useful set of images and metaphors to familiarize yourself with if you pursue dream reading. When numbers from zero to twenty-one appear in a dream, they carry the associations of the corresponding card in the major arcana of the Tarot. This can be useful information, especially if the significance of the number is otherwise obscure. And sometimes, the symbol is even clearer, as in the dream I had where the woman was making ten staffs. I interpreted it as the ten of wands (which often are large like staffs in the images). For me this was a message about nearing completion of a long project, and a warning not to give up so close to the end.

The images of the Tarot and the symbolic meanings of the cards have a long history. They continue to be popular after hundreds of years because they speak to us in a metaphorical language that reflects meaning as we bring our experiences into dialog with the images. Like an effective poem, the cards capture an understanding of human nature in symbolic language that communicates across cultures and in various spoken languages. Consider card number eight of the Major Arcana. The idea of strength is symbolized by a woman and a lion walking together. The lion represents the woman's instinctual knowledge and her own, intrinsic power. Even if the querent (the person asking a question of an oracle) is not familiar with African lions, the size and impressive mane of the lion convey the idea of strength and, at perhaps a less conscious level, the power of thought, because hair often represents thought in dreams.

Non-traditional tarot decks are also useful for readings and meditation, especially if you find a deck with art that speaks to your imagination. When in need of inspiration to sit and write, I have often pulled a card from a favorite deck and used that as my focus while I prepared for my writing session. Sometimes the image spoke to the work at hand directly, but more often, I found encouragement to continue on the creative journey, even though outward, worldly success seemed to elude me. Art, I've found, encourages art, and the process of creating art is essential to our humanity.

Here's a sample of reading Tarot cards as a comment on my life, the first Tarot spread I'd done in months:

The reading provoked a number of "ahas," especially with The Fool in the position for the *present* in the reading, and Judgment in the *outcome* position. I used *The Gilded Tarot*, which is one of my favorite decks with lush and richly-colored illustrations.

First, the Fool. In waking life, new, intriguing work possibilities had been creeping up on me. The more I taught, the more I was encouraged to teach. For several months, I'd had a deep sense of things being ready to shift, and life taking off in a new direction. And up popped the Fool in this reading. The Fool is the start of the

Tarot, the Zero card, the beginning of the journey. It's beginner's mind, as well, which synchronistically showed up in the video that my friend Cheryl Reifsnyder posted on the Wild Writers' blog just after I did my Tarot reading. The sense of awakening awareness, of innocent trust in the process; the Fool embodies all of it. When I turned over the Fool card, it felt like affirmation of everything my intuition had been telling me.

A couple of weeks before this Tarot reading, I created a new collage for my daily meditation (it hangs by my bed). The only words in it are "the call." I had been feeling the call to write, and teach, and teach through writing, pretty intensely, especially as people had been asking when I'd do more dream groups, or writing circles. The final card in the tarot reading I did was Judgment. The goddess who sounds the horn symbolizes the soul's call, its sacred contract, that which is denied at one's peril. There she was, as clear as the words on the collage. I read it as affirmation that I'm lucky to be able to hear my call so clearly, and to find my way into it fully supported by my life. The Judgment card also evoked in me the recognition that answering the call takes tenacity, awareness, and showing up, but none of those required elements is always easy. Challenges are inherent in the process.

So, like the Fool, I take the next step, always trying to get closer to answering the call that has drawn me onward this far. I'm grateful to have so many companions on the journey—the friends who have come into my life because we're all following our paths, trying to create, to dream, to increase conscious awareness.

Where to start:

You can find images from various decks online, or if you live near a store that carries tarot decks (bookstores, "New Age" stores) you can often view a sample and get a feel for the cards themselves as well as the imagery on them. I've listed some of my favorites in the "Further Reading" section.

I Ching

The I Ching is a less visual oracle than the Tarot, at least for those of us who don't immediately recognize the associations of the hexagrams with their meanings. The translation I use is the Richard Wilhelm translation, "rendered into English by Cary F. Baynes" with a forward by Carl Jung. I bought my copy used, with an inscription inside the cover that sums up the I Ching fairly well: "A book not of fortunes but advice as old as the question." As with any oracle, the querent focuses on the question as she casts coins or, more traditionally, yarrow stalks, to discover the hexagram to be used in addressing the question. Each hexagram contains six lines, determined by six throws of the coins or stalks. This brings the element of chance into the questioner's consideration, and creates a mirror of metaphor to reflect the question back to the questioner.

The Book of Changes, as the I Ching is also known, offers advice based on each hexagram. The advice is best read metaphorically, because in that way, the questioner tests it against his own understanding, listening inwardly for that "aha" that rings true. There are a lot of references to armies and warfare, thanks to the culture out of which it arose. For these metaphors, I find it helpful instead to think about gathering energy to do what I need to do, rather than a literal march against another army. These martial metaphors permeate our culture, and to our grief, some among us take them far too literally. And even though I read the passages metaphorically, I expect the military tone of the I Ching is what keeps me from turning to this ancient oracle more often than I do.

My friend Joanne though, has consulted the I Ching for over twenty years, and has a fluent relationship with it. I asked her to tell me why it appeals to her. This is her reply:

The I Ching, like dreams, speaks to just where you are at the moment. It relies on synchronicity, asking in the right moment, and openness. The more open, the more of the message that can come through. And like a dream, it is often about layers. The first hit from the I Ching is often addressing the layer closest to the surface of the question, the question you thought you were asking. Sitting with the message allows the bubbling up of deeper meaning, like swimming into the shadowy realms of the unconscious or the collective, and often reveals objects or issues that hadn't been a part of the conscious question but now seem implied or even the central inquiry of the question. The answer received, again like a dream, gives the questioner that satisfying "Aha" experience. You have learned what you needed to know, and you feel you knew it all along. The Ching is showing you your deeper knowledge. It was there all along.

I love what Joanne says about openness. It applies to every oracle and reading: "the more open, the more of the message that can come through." This openness to the message comes with practice and intent. One has to listen for the inner knowing.

And Joanne's metaphor of the "bubbling up of deeper meaning" evokes the oceans of the unconscious. When one's living consciousness engages in a conversation with a text, that conversation is happening across time, in the Invisible Realm. It's sacred ground, and miracles can happen there. Understanding, healing, insight that leads to better action—what better miracles could we wish for?

Scrying

In addition to the Tarot and the I Ching, many people turn to scrying, or seeking a message from the Invisible Realm in crystal balls, mirrors, and pools of water. Anything that presents a screen for the mind to project on offers an opportunity for the gazer to witness whatever images arise. Whether the vision is perceived as being in the crystal ball itself or contained in the imagination while gazing at the ball doesn't matter. The important thing is to witness whatever images, thoughts, or emotions make themselves known.

It may look, at first, like this form of oracle doesn't invoke the element of chance. Certainly it doesn't do so as obviously as casting coins or selecting a few cards from a deck of seventy-eight. But the moment chosen for the divination brings its own bits of randomness to the reading. What happened in the querent's life in the previous twenty-four hours will affect the querent's mind as she shapes the question and how she reads the answer. A reflective or refractive surface in a room will offer different shapes and colors to the querent's mind as she holds her mind and heart and intuition open to information about her question. Sounds or smells perceived during the scrying period might unconsciously evoke associations that the querent wouldn't otherwise have made.

These elements of chance, however, don't detract from the fact that scrying is simply a way of giving outward focus to an inner gaze. Both the Tarot and the I Ching engage the seeker with established associations of meaning for each card or hexagram. The querent reflects his own experience against the traditional meanings that arise by chance in order to come to a better understanding. Scrying in a dark pool, however, reflects the querent's mind back to him more directly, not offering anything but a still surface to project on. Like the images that pop into your head when you see a pattern in wood grain or clouds, the projections you see can tell you quite a bit about yourself. Whether they can foretell your future is for you to determine for yourself.

Pendulums

Pendulums are used to answer yes/no/maybe questions. I bought my first pendulum because I loved the stone pendant. But I do use it sometimes as an oracle. When I bought mine, I was advised to let it sit in salt for a while, so that the salt would absorb whatever energy the stone already carried. Then, the pendulum should be carried close to my body—in a pocket, for instance. The more I carry the stone, the better we communicate. I wasn't sure whether I believed this theory, but wanting to try it out properly as an oracle, I followed the instructions. When you're ready to ask your pendulum questions, start by asking it to show you how it answers yes, no, and maybe. The pendulum will stay still, or swing back and forth, side to side, or in a circle. Perhaps it will swing on a diagonal. It doesn't matter whether your yes is a circle or a back and forth swing or stationary. It only matters that you pay attention to what happens when you ask it to show you "yes." Once you're clear on what your pendulum's answers are, hold the question in your mind and the let the pendulum dangle on its chain or string and see what answer it provides.

I suspect this oracle is a way of allowing the subconscious its voice. The subtlety of the movement required of the hand or arm to make the pendulum swing gently one way or another is automatic enough to the body that we don't need to engage much consciousness to make it happen. Bypassing conscious thought in this way can give insights into what information is trying to reach us from the Invisible Realm.

Astrology

Astrology is a system of mapping the movement of the planets in our solar system and applying the symbolic meanings of the planets and their relationships on the chart to a person's life. Astrologer Catherine Woods explains it this way:

Over the years, I've noticed that many enthusiasts know astrology is a metaphorical language, but have not learned the nuts and bolts of the technical system that makes delving more deeply possible. Astrology is multi-layered, with an "alphabet" comprised of glyphs that signify signs and planets/points, and when these are "mapped" onto a pie-shaped, 12-housed chart, based on a geographic location and specific time, a basic blueprint, encoded with energetic possibility, comes to light. What is significant is that how this energetic possibility is fleshed out and given metaphorical meaning depends on the knowledge base and level of self-awareness/consciousness of the person who does this! For many, this can be quite discouraging as it can take years to learn to put the nuts and bolts together before a glimmer of the deeper metaphor at play becomes clear. Still, some will discover a passion and from there discover that many types of blueprints are possible to chart: from a natal chart, to an event chart, to a composite chart, a transit chart, a solar return chart, a progressed chart, etc.

I am a novice when it comes to astrology, yet I've had a lot of insights when I've had readings of my chart from people who are familiar with astrology's particular language. I've yet to meet an astrologer who doesn't see writing and communication as essential parts of my make-up based on my natal chart. And I've been told that one of the things my natal chart suggests is that I will be communicating knowledge of things that many people find mysterious—dreams and the Invisible Realm. Some of these readings were by people who had never met me before and knew nothing of my interests.

I've had numerous "aha" moments in dream circles where astrologers suggest relationships between dream symbols and astrological meanings. If I dream of twins, for example, Gemini might come up, and then the associations that Gemini generally carries in an astrological chart will be offered as projections on the dream.

Bibliomancy

Bibliomancy involves opening a book or magazine at random and seeing what is on the page and looking for a message in that about one's current life. If it's a large-format book, or one with dense print, you might want to randomly put a fingertip on the page to hone the message. I've used all sorts of books for this, including my own journals. I get mixed results in terms of "aha" moments, but I have had insights from this oracle.

Intuition

While scientific research has found areas of the brain associated with memory, visual input, and hearing, and has even mapped the way memories are stored in the brain, it hasn't told us how the mind works. Where does inspiration come from? Intuition? Instinct?

The brain is the powerhouse for integrating knowledge of the environment perceived by the body's senses, including intuitive awareness.

"Mommy Radar" was the first phrase I had to label intuition. This was my mom's ability to know when her kids were in (or into) trouble or needed help. Rupert Sheldrake, Ph.D., is a biologist who studies telepathy and other unexplained phenomenon. One of the things he's studied is nursing mothers whose milk lets down when they're away from their babies at the same time that the person caring for the baby notices the baby crying or waking.[10] Though the numbers of women who experience this in his survey are not overwhelming, I know very few mothers who don't feel they've had at least one instance of intuition or telepathy with their child. From an evolutionary standpoint, it would make sense that mothers who

---

[10]http://www.sheldrake.org/Articles&Papers/papers/telepathy/babies.html

are "in tune" with their children's needs would be more successful in helping their children survive to adulthood.

Intuition can be very subtle, like an uneasy feeling when meeting someone who turns out to be difficult or problematic. It can be practiced and, like dreams, seems to respond to focused attention. One way to practice is to guess who is calling on the phone before checking caller ID or answering the call. I find that my own intuitive nudges increase when I am consciously grateful for whatever guidance my intuition does provide, even, sometimes, thanking it out loud for helping me remember something or choose the right route to an event in order to avoid traffic delays.

Participating in group dream reading also fosters the development of intuition. Experienced dream readers will often have projections arise that seem unrelated to the dream at hand and may dismiss the idea without voicing it because it seems unrelated. Yet often that thought arises several times in the course of the work, and after three or four nudges, it can no longer be ignored and is finally shared with the group. These intuitive insights into the dream often provide strong "aha" moments for the dreamer.

Getting in touch with your own intuition is one of the best things you can do in life. Our society doesn't teach us how to recognize and rely on intuition. It's often labeled "women's intuition," as if it is only the province of women, and, in a patriarchal society, less valuable knowledge than empirical rationalism. It may be that women are more tuned in to intuitive knowledge, but whether that's a natural phenomenon or the result of cultural expectations is unclear. Men certainly have intuition, and successful business people will often say that they rely on it. Yet it's not a way of knowing that fits comfortably into our rationalist society, and so must be fostered privately. Perhaps one day, schools will work with students on deepening their connection with their own intuitive process.

Signs and Portents

People have been interpreting events in the natural world as signs or portents of change at least since human experience has been written down. Comets were often seen as signs that the king would die; Constantine saw a cross in the sky the night before a battle and became a Christian; people interpreted ravens as signs of death; the three Magi saw the star that led them to the manger. The modern scientific view points to such beliefs as superstition and the folly of non-scientific thinking, but like any symbol in a dream, signs and portents bear the meaning that the individual projects onto them. I'm not suggesting that drastic, impulsive action be taken based on a sign, but if the viewer has long debated an issue and asks for a sign, the sign that she notices will reflect the unconscious leanings of her mind.

All dreams have an element of portent to them, in that they show the dreamer what's to come in terms of psycho-spiritual development. But sometimes that element comes to the fore in a way that can't be ignored, as in this dream of mine: *My husband and I are on an ocean shore. Large boulders, rather than sandy beach, fill the landscape. A huge tsunami rises up, a tidal wave several stories tall. It crashes around us, yet we hold hands and run from boulder-top to boulder-top, staying just above the swirling ocean, until we reach higher ground.*

Within a year of having this dream, we weathered the declining health and deaths of a beloved pet and then both of our mothers. The tsunami symbolized the worry and grief that threatened to engulf us, and also the inundation of material goods that we inherited and the subsequent sorting and storing and donating of it all. In the depths of my grief, I often remembered this dream, and took it as a sign that together, my husband and I would eventually reach a place less tumultuous, less flooded with emotion, and we have.

Carl Jung distinguished between symbols and signs. "The sign is always less than the concept it represents, while a symbol always stands for something more than its obvious and immediate meaning."[11] According to this definition, my tsunami dream would be both a sign of the life events on the horizon and a symbol of how the event would affect my life.

The traveler to the Invisible Realm will, after careful attention, be able to discover signs that are personal to her. For instance, I take notice whenever something shows up in my life three times in a row. If three people tell me the same thing in a week, I'm going to give the information more weight than if only one does.

---

[11] Jung, Introduction to *Man and His Symbols*, p. 41.

When I came up with an idea for a creative endeavor that's far out of my comfort zone, I heard three people say an unusual word, one which is closely associated with the new project, within half an hour. I took that as a sign that I was on the right track. Other people in the room probably didn't notice the triple use of the word, because it didn't relate to their current work.

Another example of something that's both a sign and symbol for me is my pattern of seeing foxes in the waking world. In my life, foxes show up to remind me of my mom and sister, and when I'm focused on dream reading. During my mom's final decline, a fox came and sang outside my sister's window one night as she grieved. A fox sat in the parking lot at the church before Mom's memorial service, keeping vigil. Foxes appear in the backyard of my childhood home. My sister and I assign meaning to noticing them, and we notice them because we've assigned meaning to them. If I'm thinking about Mom and a fox shows up, I get the tingle that signifies I'm in touch with a more intuitive way of being in the world. And if I'm not thinking about Mom but see a fox, I think of her immediately.

Then there's the dream reading. One winter night I was on my way to a party where I'd be expected to offer ten minute dream reading appointments for a few hours. I'd never done such a thing, and I prayed on the drive over that whatever I said would be to the highest good of the hearer. I asked to be the conduit, and keep my ego out of it. I drove down a narrow, wooded street, with houses set back three times farther than in my neighborhood. I crept along, watching for the house number. A fox ran across the road, clear in the headlights but safely far away. I took it as a good sign. The evening raced by, a sure sign that I was in the zone. After the party, on my way out of the neighborhood, I saw the fox again.

The time I attended a dream work weekend led by Robert Moss, I was eager to explore the shamanistic side of dreams. The first evening, I obeyed the rules of the retreat center by going out to the parking lot to use my cell phone to call home. I sat in the rental car in the parking lot under a street lamp talking with my husband. A fox sauntered into the mostly empty parking lot about ten spaces away. It sat, watching awhile, then trotted off on its next bit of business. Another time, after I did a little dream work with a potential client, I saw two foxes traversing the space between my driveway and the neighbor's house.

Besides being markers of meaning in my waking life, foxes carry symbolic associations for me of trickster energy, cleverness, and wiliness. They are most active at dusk, and so represent crossing the realms between day and night, or waking and sleeping. They tend toward camouflage and the avoidance of trouble rather than fighting. But other people might have different associations or never see a fox at all.

Like any symbolic information that comes to the traveler in the Invisible Realm, signs and portents should be tested against the traveler's own inner knowing. Does it carry meaning for you? Does the action it encourages accord with your soul's desires? Is the action for the higher good of the traveler or the larger world? If you're taking action based on a sign, make sure that your deepest truth is in agreement.

Visits from the Dead

Nothing packs more emotion for most people than the loss of someone beloved. Death appears to be the ultimate barrier, a challenge to cross even in imagination. But across cultures around the world, the land of the dead and the land of dreams are the same place, and dreams provide one pathway for speaking with the dead, and hearing what they have to say from beyond the veil.

Sometimes the dream visitor and the message are very clear. When I offered an introduction to dreams at a local middle school, one student reported that he, his mother, and his sister, all had the same dream on the same night, in which his father, who had recently passed away, drove them all to a meadow and one at a time told them he loved them. Sometimes they are more perplexing, when the departed in the dream doesn't speak at all. (See also "Dead People" in the dream symbol appendix.)

Yet however the departed may appear, the dreamer of such dreams often takes great comfort from them. "I felt like he was telling me he was okay."

Messages arrive in other ways too. I discussed in the section on Signs that foxes became an important reminder of my mom as she was dying and continued to hold that relevance after she died. This connection received further emphasis when I read the short dreams recorded by my mom for a two month period in 1995, fourteen years before her death. In one, she dreams there is another woman with her name, a young woman, whom someone calls "Foxy."

The day after my mom's death, I returned to my own home and found that the battery in the Caller ID box had died. Within hours, the battery in the handset of our telephone also died. (Before her decline, my mother loved to talk on the phone.) While I was pondering this strange coincidence, I noticed that my next-door neighbor was jump-starting the battery on her car, which had inexplicably died. Later I learned that this is a fairly common occurrence after the death of a loved one, as if the energy of the newly-transitioned spirit is trying to get a loved one's attention.

It's a coincidence, but is it only a coincidence? Not for me. In my mind, it becomes another signpost along a pathway in the Invisible Realm; a path that takes my thoughts and feelings closer to my mom and brings me bittersweet comfort.

My sister, Karen Robinson, had the following experience after our mother's death:

With the help of hospice, my mom had a peaceful death at home. But it was still hard to let her go. Two days later I was pretty distraught. So I had an imaginary conversation with her. I said, "Oh, Mom, I'm so sorry you died. I wish I could hear you tell me it's OK." And I tried really hard to imagine her saying that it was OK. But I just couldn't get the picture to form.

The next night my husband and I were in the emergency room with my husband's dad, who had pneumonia. My husband noticed that both the nurses who were caring for his dad were named Nancy. I told the nurses that we'd scattered my mom's ashes that day, and that her name had been Nancy too.

The younger nurse gave me a strange look and said, "What was her middle name?"

I said, "Anne."

"With an E?"

I said "Yes."

She said, "My middle name is Anne. With an E." And as I stared at her, she added, "And that other Nancy over there? Also Anne. With an E."

At that point I burst into tears. And that young Nancy Anne put her arms around me, and held me close to her heart, and said, "Oh, it's OK, Sweetie. It's OK."

Stream of Consciousness

Other than dream reading, personally, my favorite path into the Invisible Realm begins in writing. There are many ways to tap into the unconscious using writing, everything from stream of consciousness in a journal to a fully crafted series of novels. Anyone who writes fiction creates a waking dream, which can hold the projections of the reader. While the writer might or might not get certain "ahas" from her own work of fiction, any reader will take the story in with more or less enthusiasm based on her own projections, and anyone can regard the story as metaphor and gather his or her own "ahas" as to the meaning of the tale. Poets, as discussed above, aim more for the single powerful metaphor than most novelists, condensing the process of arriving at the "aha." While some people are naturally gifted at these forms, they generally require the application of craft, practice, and hours of focus.

Fortunately, it's much easier than writing a novel or short story or poem, to discover the magic of writing. All it requires is to sit down to five minutes of free association. Writing prompts abound: anything in your environment can serve as a prompt, such as the vase of flowers, the cat sleeping in the sun, or a phrase taken from a newspaper, magazine, or book. These require, like scrying, the focus of attention of the mind to consider what associations arise when you consider the object or words, but that focus of the mind is only to open the tap. After that, write down what arises naturally in the mind as the associations launch you on a quick journey of free association.

As with oracles, the process can also involve chance. Through teaching process writing (as opposed to writing with a specific product in mind, like a novel) I've found that bringing together random words and images serves to get people connected with their creativity most quickly. By setting a goal of writing for ten minutes, incorporating six random words or phrases while thinking about an image, the writer must abandon the intention of being brilliant or perfect or even making sense. The goal is to just follow the trains of thought that arise and see where they lead. It can help to consider the metaphor of creating a clay pot—this is the part where the writer puts the mud on the wheel. The intention of this writing is to create the clay out of which a vase, or a coffee mug, or a bowl can be shaped.

When people engage with random words and images, creative magic happens. I've seen this over and over again in my classes. While the pieces that flow from our pens lack polish, they almost always contain nuggets of insight, wisdom, and metaphor. The more people practice this kind of free-writing, the easier the thoughts flow. This is a simple way to visit the Invisible Realm, and if done in a small group of friends, will generate shared enjoyment and "aha" moments.

Souvenirs and Stories

When we travel in the physical world, we often return home with photographs and videos, souvenirs and stories. We share our memories of the adventures we had with friends and family, but of course, our stories are not the same as the experience itself. The same is true of travels in the Invisible Realm. We can tell someone else about a dream or vision or insight, but their experience of our report will be their own, taking place in their own imaginations. We can draw or paint a picture of a dream scene, or craft a poem or novel, but these are souvenirs of the creative experience, not the experience itself.

Why bother then, to share these journeys of the imagination? Because by doing so, we invite others to experience their own journey to the Invisible Realm, gaining insight into their own interior experience and increasing understanding and compassion.

We are all on a journey through life, with its moments of ecstasy and its tragedies. We all navigate the world and yearn for meaning. When we grow in conscious awareness of who we are and what motivates us to behave one way or another, our relationships improve, our self-understanding and compassion increase, and we find meaning, even in the mundane tasks of our lives.

Here's my heartfelt wish that your travels in the Invisible Realm bring you joy and inspiration, insight and compassion. Bon voyage!

Appendix

Dreams and Dream Symbols

Introduction

What follows is an idiosyncratic exploration of dream symbols. The number of symbols dreams can use is as infinite as the known and imagined universe, so any dream symbol dictionary is necessarily limited. I've chosen to include here symbols I encounter frequently in dreams (either mine or those I hear from other dreamers), as well as ones my friends said they're curious about because they don't often appear in dream symbol dictionaries. Some of these entries appeared first on my blog, First Church of Metaphor. I share here both what I understand as common meanings of some of the symbols, as well as my personal experiences of them. I offer my projections on them with the conscious awareness that only the dreamer can say what her or his dream means. I hope you find some "aha" moments in these pages, and that these projections lead to deeper insights for you.

Architecture

When a dream focuses on architectural details or a style of architecture, I tend to project structures of belief. Is the architecture Victorian? Perhaps I, as the dreamer, am clinging to Victorian beliefs or perhaps the word brings up the idea of "victorious." Or if the dream features a large, solid, blockish building, maybe my belief systems are so solid that nothing will be able to knock them down. Or if the style is modern, with angles jutting one way and another, it might be that I've been trying to contain beliefs that appear contradictory.

Baby

Babies are symbolic of new beginnings, fresh starts, and a clean slate. That's why the New Year is represented as a baby. When a baby shows up in a dream it might be referring to a new creative project in the dreamer's life. Babies can also represent innocence and potential. When I dream of a baby I also try to see if there's any reference to my own infancy, a time when I was first learning about the world and my place in it. The dream might point to a new way I can relate to the world, or a new level of potential. Sometimes, people dream about forgetting a baby somewhere. Jeremy Taylor discusses this theme on his website, pointing out that such dreams are often about forgetting to do one's inner work, the baby representing some neglected part of the self. It's hard, sometimes, to look within and really see what part of me feels neglected, but when I do, I am able to tap into even greater joy. I can remember what it's like to look at the world with innocent joy.

Barefoot

See "Shoes, Socks, and Bare Feet"

Bees

I talked about bees in the "Meaning and 'Ahas'" section, but I'll expand on the symbolism I associate with them. Bees are very feminine, being ruled by a queen. For me, when bees show up in dreams, they bring associations with my mom and with my community of women. Because the hive acts as a cooperative organism, bees make me think of community and concern for the whole as opposed to the individual. Honey bees are also associated with the sweetness of life and the provisions given us by the Earth, or God, as in the Biblical phrase "the land of milk and honey." Unfortunately, honey bees are also currently the "canary in the coal mine" of the effect of pesticides and herbicides on our shared environment. We rely on bees to pollinate our food crops as well, so the appearance of bees in a dream suggests that there's some place in my life where I need to pay attention to a system that, if ignored and allowed to continue, might threaten my nourishment, either physical or spiritual.

Bicycle

Fairly frequently, I dream I'm riding a bicycle. Sometimes the road is smooth, but more often I'm navigating difficult terrain or riding through crowds. Sometimes, someone bumps into me, but I don't generally dream of crashing, even though I've had enough waking life experience with falling off my bike to have that sensation readily available to my mind.

Like other vehicles, bicycles are, at least at one level, about relationship. Unlike a car or bus or airplane, however, the bicycle (at least in my dreams) is built only for one, so in that sense it's about my relationship with myself. More obviously, it's about balance, and the ability to navigate life while maintaining a sense of balance. I always take such dreams as encouragement that I'm managing my life all right, even if not as perfectly as I'd like.

In my waking life, bicycles also represent an alternative to conventional ways of moving through the world. My spouse makes a habit of commuting to work by bicycle, and before an injury made riding painful for me, I strove to use my bike to get around town when I could, rather than driving. In that sense, a bicycle in a dream carries an ecological message as well, that I am (or should be) having less of a negative impact on the environment.

As professional racers endure the grueling demands of the Tour de France, I have to also consider the way a bicycle can be a vehicle for pushing oneself beyond the usual limits of physical ability. It takes courage, endurance, strength and balance to run the hard races in life. And even on the easy downhill parts of life, when the rider can coast and catch her breath, it still takes focus and balance.

Birds

I realize that trying to write about birds as a symbol is like trying to write about any large classification; the difference between dreaming of an eagle and a penguin probably trumps the similarities between them. Yet there are some generalities, at least among birds that fly, that can be discussed. As humans, we have an archetypal association between sky and heaven, and between sky and spirit. Birds, therefore, are often seen as the messengers between the mundane, everyday world and the world of spirit. Water birds bridge spirit, everyday, and the unconscious. We have this association in habits of language: "a little bird told me" is a phrase common enough to show up on greeting cards.

Not too long ago, I heard a dream from a friend that had a penguin in it. The same day, my daughter told me that a friend of hers had told her a dream with a penguin in it. The dream world tends to work this way, for those of us who hear more dreams than other people, and I always take particular notice when the same symbol comes to my attention this way, especially since before that day, I couldn't recall having ever heard a penguin dream before. My first association was with male Emperor penguins, who hold their eggs on their feet to protect them from the ice for weeks and weeks, so in my imagined version of the dream, nurturing Father energy is represented. Because penguins are excellent swimmers, they move in the ocean, a symbol of the unconscious, and so could be symbols of growing awareness of dreams and the motivations of the unconscious self.

This is a very different energy from my projections on the Steller's Jay. Jays are opportunists, stealing from people's picnics or other birds' nests. They can be loud and raucous, ruthless, and greedy, but also intelligent and visually attractive. If one shows up in my dream I want to see where I have acted in these ways. Crows are similarly intelligent, but also playful and attracted to shiny objects. Hummingbirds have strong, fast hearts, incredible speed and maneuverability, and can also be stunningly beautiful.

Of course, like any dream symbol, the meaning will depend a great deal on context. But next time you dream of a bird, consider what kind of bird it is and what qualities you associate with that kind of bird, and you'll be on your way to greater understanding.

Blue

When I dream of blue, it's usually the color of cobalt glass. Certain associations have come up so often when I've worked these dreams that they pop to mind easily. The first is the association with depression and sadness: "I'm feeling blue." But for me it is also evokes meditation and contemplation, as I have a vivid memory of being a child, lying on my back on the broad lawn of our back yard, gazing up into a summer sky. The intensity of Colorado's blue sky held me mesmerized, and ever since, blue, that nearly cobalt blue, has been my favorite color.

Cobalt itself carries an interesting association in that it is called "the goblin of the mine" because the miners found it among silver ore and considered it much less valuable. This invites the association with "goblin of the mind," or negative self-talk.

Blue is also linked to the throat chakra in that system of understanding, and so has to do with using my voice. In that sense it has to do with teaching.

Blue ribbons signify first place, and "blue blood" refers to the elite in society. So when I dreamed of finding a cobalt-blue sphere that allowed me to become lucid, my dream offered a symbol of my most valued, most talented part of myself leading the way into conscious awareness.

Blue's association with the sky also makes it a metaphor for the divine, as many cultures associate the heavens with the sky.

Boat

One of the dreams I had the good fortune to work in one of Jeremy Taylor's dream circles contained the image of a toy blue boat that I owned as a child. I received it on my fourth birthday and it's still knocking around the house of dreams. Boats remind me of my mom, who spent her childhood playing in water. The presence of a little girl in the dream offers me the parent's perspective. Both of these associations make me think of the ways my role as a mother is changing as my daughters grow, the praise and grief of watching them need me less. What will I do with myself? The creative life is chomping at the bit, bringing with it the fear of tapping into it at the rate it seems to want.

But the projection also came up in the circle that the blue boat I'm riding in this life is depression. With that projection came the reminder that meeting life with an open heart enables me to overcome the depression.

In idiom, we speak of "my ship coming in" to denote great success, usually after long labor, or "that ship has sailed" to speak of an opportunity that has passed. Boats have ancient and archetypal associations as well, including the womb and cradle, the voyage of life, birth and death. A boat provides a thin barrier between a person and the water, and so is a symbol of safety in the presence of great danger, and of riding the currents of life. According to Taschen's *The Book of Symbols*, included in its metaphorical meanings, "The boat denotes those things, material, spiritual, energetic, that suddenly appear on our horizons and are brought to shore." [12]

---

[12] *Book of Symbols*, p. 450.

In the dream I shared at the workshop, the toy boat also carries associations of play and innocence, when I could live life "merrily, merrily, merrily, merrily," and life did feel like a dream.

Bones

When bones appear in dreams, there is often a reference to ancestors and resurrection, since bones are the last part of the body to decompose after death. Many cultures preserve the bones of their ancestors in one way or another, and some religions hold on to the bones of those they consider saints in the belief that such relics can perform miracles. Bones can refer to something true at the psychic core, as when we say, "I knew it (or felt it) in my bones."

The marrow of a bone is often a metaphor for the truth or useful information at the core of a situation. Marrow can also be removed, leaving a hollow bone. My friend Suzanne Rougé speaks of her desire to be a "hollow bone" for the divine, meaning the desire to remove ego from the action and just work on behalf of divine will. A hollow bone can also be played as a flute, which reinforces the symbol of letting the divine "play" through me in order to make beautiful music.

A skull and crossbones represents poison and death, as well as pirates.

There's also the sexual reference of a "boner" being an erect penis.

"Broken Pelvis"

This is a more thorough exploration of the dream I mentioned at the beginning of the book, with some text repeated here for clarity:

I'm standing at the counter of a hotel. My pelvis is broken in three places and there is no clerk to help me. I think, "I have to sit down," but immediately amend that to "I have to get off my pelvis." I will have to lie on the floor. The counter is now simultaneously the hotel counter and my kitchen counter. The pain is unbearable.

I brought this dream to a circle at Billie Ortiz's Dream Retreat during the Chainsaw/Hummingbird portion of the work. (That's where we offer a single symbol or narrowly focused dream and people project on it for about 10 or 15 minutes.) My emotional state was pretty clear in the broken feeling of the dream: my mother and my mother-in-law were suffering from the illnesses that would take them both from me in the next nine months. I'd grieved so much already that those emotions were right at the surface. I'd also had pain in my hip in waking life for about five months when I had the dream.

I had a lot of "aha" moments from the group's projections—the pelvis evoking motherhood, the breaks evoking grief. The fact that there was no one behind the counter suggests that there is no gatekeeper to stop me from going to this profoundly painful place. The projection that unleashed the tears was that I was somehow, in a shamanic way, helping these women I loved bear the pain they were suffering. When I got home and told my husband about the experience, he suggested that the third break in the dream could be our ancient cat, Tilki, whose weight loss and fragility echoed my mom's physical condition in profound and eerie ways. All three of these females had weakness and instability in their pelvises. The three breaks in my dream made perfect, painful sense.

Three years after I experienced the dream, my understanding of it continued to unfold. For a few months I'd been helping my aunt transition from independent living to a care facility. At some point the dream came to mind and I realized that she is the third woman of the generation above mine who was an important part of my family life. So now in my understanding of the dream she shares the third break with my cat, which is also fitting because my aunt's elderly female cat had to come live with me when my aunt moved out of her house.

The hip and back pain never fully left me in the years since the dream. The most relief I've found has come through my friend Kim Hansen's compassionate Feldenkrais work. Throughout the challenging process of assisting my aunt, Kim made herself available to help me literally unwind the torqued positions I got into. One of the metaphors we worked with is the impulse to both stop and go, and I was thinking of "breaks on the pelvis" when the light bulb went on and I thought "brakes on the pelvis." The "aha" gave me chills, as I realized that I have profound resistance to plunging into the grief that my aunt's life situation is awakening. Yet I know that the only way out is through, and I try to listen to my body when it demands that I move, or stop moving to just be. Just lie down with my grief and pain.

(See also "Bones")

Cannibalism

This is an intriguing symbol, and not one I've encountered very much. So I'll start with a theoretical piece about eating in dreams in general, which has resonated for me. Since we don't need to eat in the dream world, when we do eat, the act has symbolic significance. I've learned a lot about this idea from Jeremy Taylor, who discusses eating in dreams on his blog at Psychology Today. [13] I find an "aha" from his suggestion that eating in dreams can symbolize fully taking something in, integrating it into myself so that it is no longer something separate. Like so many things in life, that can have apparently paradoxical meanings. It can be a good sign that I've fully integrated some learning or experience, and it could indicate that I've taken in beliefs about myself that may or may not be true.

When I imagined cannibalism for myself, I thought about how our first nourishment in this world comes directly from the mother's body. In the womb, we take in nutrients through her blood. We may have continued to eat from her body after birth, by drinking her milk, though that's not literally true for every baby, since

---

[13] http://www.psychologytoday.com/blog/the-wisdom-your-dreams/201101/eating-in-dreams

formulas were and still are used to substitute or supplement breast milk. But in utero, we were all, in a sense, cannibalistic. So the image for me represents those introjects, or beliefs about myself that came from outside of myself, which I received from my mother. Her fears, her joys, her attitude about being pregnant…all of these were emotions I experienced while in her body. Whatever these emotions imprinted on me might still be at the foundation of some belief I have about myself. The graphic horror of the dream image gets my attention in a big way, so this is something I need to know about myself.

The devouring mother is also an archetypal symbol—the Great Mother both gives birth and devours her children. So there's a resonance for me with cannibalism in the dream, that I am experiencing something in my life that feels like the energy of the devouring mother. It's an inexorable and inevitable process to grow and change and affect those around us in our lives, and the changes that take place sometimes are difficult to process, and may feel as repulsive as cannibalism. Challenges in life like the loss of a loved one, the shifting relationship to one's family, the loss of a job, or a physical challenge, may be represented by the cannibalism in the dream. If I eat something, I have to process it; to take what nourishment I can from it and let go of the rest. That process can be difficult, even repugnant from my ego's point of view, as it will inevitably change the way I understand myself, and the world. And so the dream may choose something I find repugnant in waking life to show me the hard work I've been doing.

Cars

Cars show up frequently in my dreams, and I've come to look at them in several ways: as a symbol of how I'm moving through the world, as a symbol of myself in motion, and as a symbol of relationship. Of course, the question of where I am in the car will yield some information about whether I feel in control (comfortably in the driver's seat) or along for the ride (elsewhere in the car) or in conflict (trying to drive from the back seat, for example). If I'm sliding with no traction, the dream may be telling me there's nothing to do but ride this out, or it may be illustrating how very out-of-control a situation has become.

One image with cars came up a lot when I was exploring my chronic pain. The image is having one foot on the brake and the other on the gas. I've had this dream experience, so it's easy to evoke, but I was experiencing it at a primarily intellectual level, thinking about how I have both the urge to move forward and the urge to stop myself. Then I tried an experiment, where I pushed against a piece of furniture with my left foot as hard as I could—the braking foot if I'm braking and accelerating at the same time. A sense of utter desperation flooded me—the primal urge to hang on to this moment of life, to stop the changes I see coming, to keep those I love close beside me when I know that time will inevitably take them away. The emotional response was profound, and at the same time cathartic, as I recognized that I can't stop any of the change, so I might was well jump in and ride it.

Not that I think I've found the answer, but the moment was healing in that I recognized a mostly unconscious urge and now can look at it in the light of consciousness. Recognizing the contrasting impulses, and honoring the emotion behind them both, helps me sort out exactly what it is that I really want and how I'll deal with what life throws my way.

Cats

At one of Billie Ortiz's dream retreats, we heard a dream in which a black panther appeared. Being black, the panther could represent night and shadow, and being a wild cat, represents predatory instincts. In a dream of mine from several years ago, a male African lion paced around a ballroom with a cut paw, leaving blood on the floor. My associations with lions include courage/cowardice (because of the Cowardly Lion from the Wizard of Oz) and royalty (King of the Jungle).

I dream fairly often of domestic cats as well, and as pets, they can represent unconditional love and compassion. Cats as a whole also represent instinctive, intuitive knowledge, careful observation, patience, pouncing at the right moment, self-grooming, and fastidiousness. If the cat is a wild cat, it will represent my untamed, wild instinctive energies, while a domesticated cat represents those same energies contained and tamed.

One difference between domestic cats and most wild cats is the ability to purr. As a human, I can't purr (though I've often tried to mimic the sound) but metaphorically, dreaming of a small cat suggests the ability to use vibrational energy within my own body to soothe myself and others and to show contentment and pleasure. This might look more literally like singing or chanting, or it might manifest as choosing positive self-talk over negative.

Many cats have the ability to move silently. If I'm lying in bed with my eyes closed, I will always hear my cat Finn jump up to join me, but I very rarely hear my cat Grayson. I won't know Grayson is there until he sniffs my face. So if I dream of Grayson, that stealthy ability would be one of the associations I'd consider when unpacking the dream.

Of course, each dreamer will have her or his own associations with cats, some positive and some negative. I still bear the scar of having intervened in a cat fight that was taking place through a window screen. My arm's movement triggered all the anticipated fighting moves in my gentle and timid Tasha, and her rear foot raked over my elbow leaving a gash about five inches long. It got infected and left a ragged scar, which has now, twenty-five or thirty years later, shrunk and faded a little but is still quite visible. It serves as a reminder that I have that fierce energy inside myself as well, and if I must, I can protect myself, though I hope I'll be able to distinguish in the moment before I lash out between those who wish me harm and those who are trying to help.

Cave

When I imagine caves for myself, they are dark and mysterious places, a perfect metaphor for going within to rest, to dream, and to learn what wisdom lies within. I picture a bear, or other wild animal, finding a cave to sleep most of the winter away, letting the mind explore through dreams rather than waking experience. So caves in dreams are, for me, self-referential, or a meta-level comment on the dream, its presence an invitation to me to remember that I'm dreaming.

Because I tend to equate hibernation in caves with bears, even though I know other animals hibernate, if a cave shows up in my dream, I'll likely ask myself if I've been acting like a bear lately, Mama or Papa or Cub. That makes me remember that bear cubs are born in the depth of winter, born of dreams. Is there a part of me that is newly born?

Because hibernation is a long sleep, and sleep for me is about dreams and healing and integration, a cave evokes that sense of taking time to heal, to integrate, and to let the dreams speak. Time to rest. Every winter, I get a few days of feeling so miserable from some head cold that the only reasonable thing to do is rest. It's hard to learn to take the time to rest first, before the misery hits, but if I forget my body is willing to remind me. Illness is a "cave" time for me.

Of course, caves that hold darkness hold the unconscious. My fears lie in those shadows, as do the very gifts I need to stay conscious to larger patterns and bigger purposes than my human self tends to notice on a quotidian basis. So a cave in a dream is an invitation to explore my shadow self, to look deeply into the parts of myself that I like to believe it would be easier to ignore. In truth, if I ignore them too long, they will get my attention, through feathers or bricks. I always pray to be awake enough to notice the feather.

(See also "The Corpse in the Cave")

Clocks

See "Time and Clocks"

Clothing

I know some dreamers who have such detailed recall they can describe what everyone in the dream is wearing. For me, I generally only recall clothing when I (as the viewpoint character) or another character in the dream is wearing something distinctive. I remember one dream from several years ago in which I walk down a hill in the middle of the street with Bill Murray. I'm wearing bright yellow overalls with paint splatters on them, and he gives me a handful of coins.

If I actually owned bright yellow overalls, the meanings might be different, but since these were straight out of the dream costume shop, I paid close attention to trying to understand their significance. I explored all my associations with that color yellow and the paint splatters on the clothes. My dream invited me to be more confident and "showy" in my artistic endeavors.

Clothing, as a metaphor, represents the way we present ourselves to the world. If the dreamer is usually a conservative dresser and the dream shows wild or revealing dress with no one else in the dream acting shocked or surprised, it might mean that the dreamer can show a wider range of self-expression without offending social norms. Or if I notice that my dinner companion in the dream is wearing a shirt that looks old-fashioned, perhaps I've been sitting with an old-fashioned idea or attitude.

Dreaming of wearing costumes adds another layer of meaning to the idea that clothes represent the way I show myself to the world. A costume suggests that I'm pretending to be something or someone that I'm not, or that there's some part of me needing expression that is alien to who I think I am.

Clouds

For many years, I've found great pleasure in photographing clouds, especially sunsets. This has become such a part of my life that it has shown up in my dreams; in one dream I was taking a photo of a sunset near a barn and a great eye appeared in the cloud. Sometime later, a waking life cloud reminded me of the dream. But even without the extra imagery of a dream, clouds speak to some non-verbal part of my spirit.

I find comfort and delight in the various patterns and colors, as well as in the movement when they ride rivers of air.

Clouds help us see the movement of the unseen, and so in that sense serve as a metaphor for consciousness of the Invisible Realm. They are made of moisture, whether or not they release that moisture to the earth, and so are symbolic of emotion. We use "stormy" to describe a mood, and poor Eeyore always has his own gloomy cloud following him around. In many cultures, clouds are associated with fertility because of their life-giving rains.

One of the simplest games of childhood is to see images in clouds as our minds search for patterns in the randomness of a chaotic system. This is a good way to think about projection, for one person might see a bird with wide wings and another sees a mother with outstretched arms, and a third perceives a crucifix.

Clouds are paradoxical as well, being both ephemeral in the moment but part of an eternal cycle. And for me, they represent the idea that the gifts of spirit are available equally to everyone.

Cobwebs

A few years after my mother died, I dreamed of going up into an upper floor bedroom and the upper part of the doorway was shrouded in old cobwebs. My first reading on it was that there's some place in my head that was feeling cobwebby and unattended.

I'm sure other dreamers would project other layers of meaning on the cobwebs in that space. Another possibility is that, since spiders are often associated with the Great Mother, and so by extension mothers in general, maybe these cobwebs, old and tattered, represented the grieving process I'd gone through since my mother died. The cobwebs in the dream don't bother me, they're just something I notice as I go through the doorway. That's how my grief felt when I had the dream—familiar but not encumbering.

Consort

When I was a child, my mom told me that before I was born, she'd hoped I'd be twins, because she wanted to have another child but couldn't endure another pregnancy. The idea gave metaphorical birth to an imaginary sibling, one who would take my side when my older siblings told me I was too young. I imagined a brother, because that would balance out the family nicely. He's been my imagined companion in this life ever since.

The following dream, which I had in my mid-twenties, when I was an Assistant Big Fish in a Small Town Pond, reinforced my twin's presence in the life of my mind.

"The Corpse in the Cave"

I am in the doorway of a cave, facing inward. The light is very dim, and I approach the back wall, on alert as I face the darkness. I reach a corpse. I stand beside it. The body is swathed in white, the uncovered face to my left, and as I look closer, I see that it's more decayed than I first thought.

I turn away in a surge of horror and alarm, and flee. But before I reach the cave's threshold, I remember that I'm supposed to turn and face my fear. I stop, with the awareness of the corpse and the fear crowding into my back.

I face the corpse.

It has vanished, replaced by an angel of light, tall and so magnificent that I have to squint.

"I'm Michael," he says, "I wanted to be with you in this life, but I couldn't." Love, the most accepting love I'd ever known, washed through me from Michael, accompanied by the assurance that he wanted to be with me in the physical world, and bittersweet grief that he wasn't.

The dream has stayed with me, a clearer memory than many from my waking life. I've found Michael's company again and again through hypnotherapy and dreams and imaginings. Whether he is real isn't even a question. He is a very real being who lives in my imagination. In my mid-twenties, with my mom reminding me that women my age were less likely to get married, the knowledge that Michael had wanted to live during my life had the tragic quality of romance-out-of-reach. Then I planned my big move, to graduate school, and before I left Small Town Pond I dreamed this:

I am in College Town, in front of a small house in a quiet neighborhood. Michael is there, sitting in a young maple tree, gazing down at me fondly.

I don't remember now if we spoke. If I went digging through my archives, I could probably find the original notes about the dream, but no guarantees—my journals were hodgepodge then. But it doesn't matter, because a few years later, my fiancé and I bought a house with a young maple tree that looked very much like the house in my dream. I knew I had Michael's blessing, and he felt comfortable, without the romantic projection.

As I got into dream work, I projected onto my imagined Michael the archetype of Consort, Jeremy Taylor's elegant choice for removing gender from Jung's idea of Animus and Anima. The Consort is that energy that complements ours—what we metaphorically see as masculine or feminine energy. So for me, a heterosexual woman, the complementary energy, or my Consort, is a heterosexual man. My dreams keep bringing to my attention this meeting of the energy I habitually employ less, but now need. The integration of the masculine and feminine seems to me the next big step in how we imagine gender. By recognizing that we all share both energies, we allow for people to be who they are, in all their glorious, cheerful diversity. Where we fall on the spectrum of human characteristics is unique to each of us, so we might as well accept that other people will experience life a little, or a lot, differently than we will, and get over ourselves and on with the work of creating a world in which we all belong.

For me, the steps to doing that include facing my fears (which is harder in waking life than in dreams), honoring my imagination's version of the energies I need in my life, and allowing the sense of spiritual support that Michael offers to really come in to my psyche.

(See also "Cave")

"The Corpse in the Cave"
See "Consort"

Crying
See "Laughter and Crying"

Dancing

I've dreamed I was waltzing with a beloved dance teacher who passed away years ago, that I was setting up speakers to dance with extended family in empty spaces in an airport parking garage, and dreamed of dancing that felt like flying. For me, dancing is associated with times of pure enjoyment, of the youthful joy of having a body that moved with grace and without pain, and of the stage fright and excitement of performing as a child.

When I dream of dancing, I think about community, especially if it's a circle dance, and of partnership if it's a couple dance. As a metaphor, dancing with someone means engaging with that person with a kind of formal intimacy. Dance is a form of self-expression, so to dream of dancing could be an encouragement to express myself in a way that doesn't involve words (a challenge for a writer). Dancing is also something I do with my whole body, so to dream of dancing is a reminder to return to greater body awareness, to focus on how I move and where my body reacts with the desire to protect and hold, and where it freely moves.

There's something extremely satisfying about dancing in groups, everybody moved by the same music, the same rhythm. Cultures all over the world use community dance to celebrate life transitions or just to have fun. I wonder if the joy found in moving as part of a larger group of dancers is akin to the sensation of being part of a flock of birds moving in synchronized movement, or of fish swimming in schools.

I didn't train professionally to be a dancer, but if I had, dancing in dreams would carry associations of discipline and self-sacrifice in addition to whatever joy came from mastering movement as an art form.

For me, dancing in dreams is always a reminder to dance more in my waking life. It's one of life's simplest pleasures.

Dead people

A few years ago I had the privilege of speaking to some students who were around 12 and 13 years old about dreams. Among the many questions they had about dream symbols, a few wanted to know about the appearance in their dreams of loved ones who had died. The dreams I heard reported that day were comforting, despite re-awakening grief. One girl dreamed that a friend who had been killed in a car accident had appeared to say good-bye. Another reported a dream shared by his mother, his sister, and himself, that his deceased father had taken them all on a car ride into the mountains, stopped at an overlook and then spoken to each of them privately, telling them he was okay and they should take care of each other.

The question these students had for me was whether their loved ones had actually been present, or whether it was "just a dream," a construct of their minds like their nighttime dreams.

How to answer such a question? I'd had my share of such dreams. When I moved to a new town, I began having dreams of a high school friend who had attended college there. I'd heard, years earlier, that she had a brain tumor, but had lost track of her and didn't know if she was still alive. I began to have dreams in which she appeared and my overwhelming need in the dream was to find out where she was in waking life, so that we could reconnect. I asked, over and over, "Where are you?" but she never answered. I always woke from these dreams with grief and longing. It was the early days of the Internet, and I tracked down a phone number. I called, and reached her mother, who told me my friend had died several years earlier. After that, I had one more dream about her, where I was lucid enough to know she was dead and could converse with her holding that knowledge in mind. She never showed up in my dreams again.

Was her spirit trying to communicate, to say good-bye? Or were these dreams that arose from my own psyche as a way to process the loss of my friend? Clearly, there's no way to answer that empirically, but my sense is that she was really there. The dreams had a different feel to them than ordinary dreams, a luminosity and intensity of emotion that surpassed any dreams I'd had up until that point.

What I told the students who asked me about the dreams of their loved ones was that no one could say for certain, but that I certainly believe spirits of the dead are able to communicate with us in dreams. My answer only confirmed what these children already suspected, that their dreams had been true communication. Of course, only the dreamer can say for sure what his or her dream means, but when I offered my opinion the students had that sense of "aha," and "yes, that's so."

I've had many dreams of those I loved, some feeling just like dreams, others feeling like actual interactions with my loved ones' spirits. While I can find metaphorical meaning even in the true visitation dreams, I choose to believe what my heart tells me is so, that in those blessed moments, my loved ones have come to say hello.

Death

One of the most disturbing metaphors that dreams employ is that of death. A friend recently wrote to me after he dreamed that his son had died. The dream had been so vivid that he couldn't shake the despair of it all day. As a metaphor, death represents, in Jeremy Taylor's words, "profound psycho-spiritual growth and change." Whatever dies in the dream represents that part of the dreamer that has changed so much that death is the only adequate metaphor. If the death in the dream is accidental, unintended, then I as the dreamer am changing in less than conscious ways. But if the dream is of suicide, then I've consciously pursued the change that the dream illustrates.

The problem with suicide dreams is that if they are taken literally, the dreamer may think the subconscious is actually recommending suicide as an option. This mistaken literalism gets in the way of understanding what the dream is trying convey, which is that change is necessary for spiritual growth. Even waking thoughts of suicide shouldn't be taken literally, but only metaphorically. One of the great dream work teachers, Robert A. Johnson, used to say, "By all means, kill yourself, but do not harm your body." It's hard to reinvent ourselves, but it's possible. Maybe all that's needed is to find a creative outlet, or to pursue a creative outlet I already know with even more passion. I've been suicidal and I know how hard it is to think clearly, much less metaphorically, when all my inner demons have come out to play. But if I had known then what I know now, perhaps I would have sought ways to transform my life experience in a drastic, but non-lethal way.

A few months ago, a young woman wrote to me out of concern for her friend, who had had thoughts of suicide and dreamed often of an angelic being that came to her and took her flying. She also had dreams of being outside her body. The young woman who wrote was worried that her friend was seeing the dreams as an affirmation of her self-destructive thoughts. I offered this response:

Flying dreams for me are often about creativity and my ability to express it in the world—a very good sign, if I'm flying. Having an angel by my side would suggest to me that my higher self is encouraging me to express my creativity. It's often in creative acts that I get out of my worst funks and lose myself in the work. In my imagined version of this dream, the angel has come to remind me that I have freedom to be who I truly am here on this planet.

The out of body dream for me is a similar reminder that the life of the soul/spirit/higher self is eternal, and that the peace is available to me on this plane as well. I certainly understand the appeal of suicide—I've been in that space many times in my life—but I also know that something always comes along that makes me glad I stuck around, and that my work in this life isn't done. If I had a dream where I experienced the profound peace described in your friend's dream, I'd be encouraged (literally, filled with courage) to continue this life and endure its struggles knowing that the peace awaits me at the end. I know it's hard to get through the days and nights sometimes, but with the advantage of being in my mid-life, I also know that the days and nights pass by faster and faster and that each day gives me some reason I'm glad to be here, even if it's just seeing a flower in bloom or a beautiful sunset, or being able to hold the door open for someone who's struggling more than I am. So if I were your friend, I'd take the dream as a sign that I can touch that greater consciousness of the universe (God, the Divine, whatever you want to call it) and take comfort in knowing that my higher self has given me this dream to comfort me.

Dreams of suicide and death are often disturbing and can have the impact of a nightmare. They get our attention. They're asking us to find creative ways to change, to endure a metaphorical death. Or perhaps they're showing us that we've already endured it. Either way, the subtext is always, "but do not harm your body."

(See also "Dolmen")

Dolmen

A dolmen is a Neolithic stone tomb, usually with two side stones and a capstone that spans the distance between the side stones. They were, in some cases at least, covered with soil, which has weathered away. They could be considered portals to the afterlife. As a dream symbol, they carry associations with death (transformation) and access to the Invisible Realm. As tombs, they symbolize, for me, the idea that something of myself is entombed, that is, buried in a way that feels permanent and unchanging. The stones evoke the appearance of permanence but also the suggestion that anything built by humans eventually gives way to the passage of time, as stone walls crumble and even dolmens eventually fall. I can't escape the pun of "dole men"—so maybe my masculine aspect is "on the dole" somehow, living off the efforts of my feminine side without offering work in exchange.

(See also "Death")

Elephant

Probably the first association with elephants that comes to many people's minds is the phrase "An elephant never forgets." The long memory of elephants shows up in dreams when we are invited to recall something we may have put away in some corner of our minds. Or to show us how the problem we're dealing with now is connected to a memory.

We also talk about "the elephant in the room," meaning a problem or situation that is big and obvious but that people are ignoring out of a reluctance to deal with the problem. So if an elephant shows up in a room in a dream, I'd be curious what problem the dreamer is trying to ignore.

Elephants are highly intelligent, self-aware, and exhibit a full range of emotions. Depending on the context of the dream, elephants remind us that we are not the only sensate beings on the planet. Because of their size, elephants remind us that we too have great capacity for the full spectrum of qualities they have.

The elephant-headed god Ganesh is the remover of obstacles. It's easy to see how elephant energy would be associated with removing obstacles, as the size and strength of the animals makes it easy for them to clear a path for themselves if necessary. So if a dream shows just an elephant's head, this association would be particularly strong.

A white elephant has come to mean an unwanted gift, after the tradition of kings giving white elephants to courtiers who offended them. The animal was too rare and prized to be anything but an expensive pet, and the recipient would have to spend a lot of wealth on its upkeep. Metaphorically, this could be a talent that is unused, thereby costing the dreamer too much energy to keep it idle, or it could be an unwanted responsibility wrapped in the guise of an honor.

The elephants in my dreams are often figurines, rather than live animals, and so invite me to examine in what ways the qualities of the elephant are trivialized and used only for decoration in my life.

Then of course, there is the metaphor expressed in the story of the six blind men and the elephant, in which each man takes hold of a different part of the elephant and concludes that the entire elephant is the part. The version of this tale that I like best is by the 19th-century poet John Godfrey Saxe:

> It was six men of Indostan
> To learning much inclined,
> Who went to see the Elephant
> (Though all of them were blind),
> That each by observation
> Might satisfy his mind.
>
> The First approached the Elephant,
> And happening to fall
> Against his broad and sturdy side,
> At once began to bawl:
> "God bless me!—but the Elephant
> Is very like a wall!"

The Second, feeling of the tusk,
Cried: "Ho!—what have we here
So very round and smooth and sharp?
To me 'tis mighty clear
This wonder of an Elephant
Is very like a spear!"

The Third approached the animal,
And happening to take
The squirming trunk within his hands,
Thus boldly up and spake:
"I see," quoth he, "the Elephant
Is very like a snake!"

The Fourth reached out his eager hand,
And felt about the knee.
"What most this wondrous beast is like
Is mighty plain," quoth he;
"'Tis clear enough the Elephant
Is very like a tree!"

The Fifth, who chanced to touch the ear,
Said: "E'en the blindest man
Can tell what this resembles most;
Deny the fact who can,
This marvel of an Elephant
Is very like a fan!"

The Sixth no sooner had begun
About the beast to grope,
Than, seizing on the swinging tail
That fell within his scope,
"I see," quoth he, "the Elephant
Is very like a rope!"

 And so these men of Indostan
Disputed loud and long,
Each in his own opinion
Exceeding stiff and strong,

Though each was partly in the right,
And all were in the wrong!

So, oft in theologic wars
The disputants, I ween,
Rail on in utter ignorance
Of what each other mean,
And prate about an Elephant
Not one of them has seen!

The metaphor here is that the elephant is to the blind men as God is to humans. We only glimpse one small part at best, and make our assumptions and projections about the rest.

"Fire Prediction"

In September of 2008 I attended a workshop led by Robert Moss. We explored dreams and played in the Invisible Realm by peering into the future through trance states. In one exercise, we took a group journey to see what we could of 2012. It takes some trust for me to let visions unfold in a situation like this, without second-guessing what I see. It's a lot like writing that way. After we came back from our visions we reported to the group what we'd seen and subsequently sent them by email to one group member as a record. Here's some of what I saw:

First I see a big fire in Kansas. There is drought along the Front Range of Colorado. Horsetooth Reservoir near Fort Collins, CO, is nearly empty. A big storm hits Laramie, Wyoming, causing flooding. Obama is in office. There's a focus on solar and wind energy—lots of development.

Clearly not all of it came true in 2012, and those parts that did weren't hard to predict. Obama's election was by no means certain in September of 2008, but it seemed likely. And forecasting drought for the Front Range of Colorado in any given year has better than 50-50 odds. The rest seems like I got it wrong, but with the High Park fire in June of 2012 near Horsetooth Reservoir west of Fort Collins, I had an "aha" when I returned to this prediction and read it instead as a metaphorical experience.

The High Park fire consumed places I visited frequently in my childhood, transforming them in dramatic ways. The land will recover, since fire is a natural process in forests, but for years after such a fire, the trees will be only blackened trunks. The animals that lived there, if they survived, have to find new homes until the habitat can regenerate. Fire is the ultimate transformative element, and in that sense, as a dream symbol, carries much the same weight as death.

Kansas, as a symbol, has a primary association for me as the childhood home of Dorothy in *The Wizard of Oz*. In the movie, it is the land of the ordinary, shown in black and white and gray, while the land of Oz is shown in color. Dorothy learns a great deal about herself and about friendship during her travels in Oz, and even though she returns to her childhood home, she's no longer the child she was when the tornado carried her off. For me, the image in my vision of Kansas burning is a metaphor for my childhood burning away. The summer of 2012 saw places of my childhood changing in dramatic ways, not just with the fire but also with the home of a relative being cleared out and prepared to go on the market. When I entered that house that summer, memories of family holiday dinners bumped up against the sadness of inevitable change and the reminder that those days are gone forever except in memory. As the generation above me slips away, I have fewer places to stand where I'm the "child" and more and more have to be present as the adult.

I learned a lot about myself and my friends in this process, and the daily dose of wildfire smoke in the air served as a constant reminder that the only way to go home again is in my imagination.

"Five or Six"

Often in my dreams and in dreams I've heard, the dreamer will report that there were "five or six" of something, such as "five or six people in the room," or "five or six feet away." It seems an insignificant detail, a bit of dream not quite remembered precisely. Yet the dream could choose anything to put in there. I could, for example, be sure it's five people, or three people, or thirty. I could know that the box is exactly six inches wide. The uncertainty isn't accidental, and in fact carries a meaning that to my mind is always worth bringing up when discussing the dream.

As humans, we have our usual five senses—sight, hearing, taste, touch, and smell. What we refer to as the sixth sense are usually psi abilities like psychic knowing, telepathy, or deep and expansive intuition. Body workers might argue that the sixth sense is balance, or there could be a number of other, alternative sixth senses, like proprioception (the sense of how one's body is oriented in space).

When the dream offers the option of "five or six" it's worth asking the dreamer whether a sixth sense has been employed, or could be employed. Or, whether it's even recognized by the dreamer.

For me, five and six has other, very personal meanings. Five always evokes my family of origin, which had five members. So when five shows up in a dream, I consider the possibilities of childhood roots for the situation the dream illustrates for me. And six has been my lucky number since I was six years old. So for me, six is a very personal number, a number that makes me think of how I am an individual and different from the other members of my family. When "five or six" shows up in a dream then, one question that is always present for me is whether I'm viewing the problem from the point of view I was raised to have, or the point of view that is true at my core. Depending on the situation, they may be the same, or they may be very different.

Flying

Flying dreams are, for me, often a symbol for the desire for more creative expression. If we are, indeed, created in "God's image," my understanding is that the way in which we are most like the divine energy that permeates the universe is in our urge to create. We, as humans, are innately creative. It's what has enabled everything from soaring musical compositions to the technological domination of the planet. Yet many of us subsume our creative energies because they don't fit neatly into our 9 to 5 lives, and if we do, our dreams will come to urge us to find ways to express ourselves. Flying in dreams is both a reminder that the urge is there and a celebration of any recent waking life attempts to give that creative urge a voice. Flying is also the ability to defy gravity, which is one of the laws of the physical world that we all must live with. In that sense, flying is about escaping from conventional rules about how to live.

Flying is also very bird-like, and so represents the ability to move between the mundane and the spiritual realms, and perhaps bring knowledge back from the spiritual realm into everyday life.

(See also "Death")

Gender and Transgender

As women's roles shifted in the twentieth century and continue to change today, gender shows up a lot in dreams. Many dream readers, following Jungian thought, identify masculine energy as the initiatory force in a creation while the feminine is the more receptive, gestating energy. This dichotomy is useful from a symbolic point of view, even though all humans have both kinds of energy, often on a shifting continuum. Dreams can help us understand those energies in ourselves and how they're working together or against one another. The symbols may arise as groups dominated by one gender or the other, or may show up as men with female sex organs or vice versa. They may call attention to themselves through transvestism. As our society grapples with the erosion of patriarchy in favor of something more balanced, these sorts of dreams will continue to arise.

I hear a lot more dreams from women than from men, so my sample is skewed, but I've heard many dreams in which the female dreamer dreams she's a man and not many at all from men who've dreamed of being a woman. However, I expect that similar themes are at play in both versions of this dream. I've had many dreams of being a man. Sometimes this is just a knowing I have in the dream, like one where I was chasing a streetcar. All the focus was outward, trying to catch the streetcar, but I clearly knew that I was a man in the dream. In other dreams, the focus is on the distinguishing anatomy, which carries further levels of association.

For the first kind of dream, for me the knowledge that I'm a man in the dream suggests that I'm integrating masculine and feminine roles or energies. While it's a metaphorical construct to define masculine as action oriented and decisive and feminine energy as receptive and nurturing, it can be a useful construct for examining this type of dream. If I dream I'm the opposite sex, perhaps I'm discovering parts of myself that I somehow feel "belong" with the opposite anatomy. One suggestion is to make a list of qualities, faults, and characteristics you associate with "men" and "women" and to see what on that list feels comfortable and familiar and what feels more alien. Which characteristics come into play in the dream?

To dream specifically of genitalia can of course carry all sorts of personal associations, but on a more archetypal level, the penis is associated with the power to impregnate, to provide the spark that brings something to life. It suggests potency and the ability to take action. The vulva is receptive and/or devouring, the gateway of birth and blood. Depending on the context of the dream, of course, this suggests the ability to take something in and nurture it until it's ready to enter the world.

Hair

Hair on my head in a dream often refers to my thoughts, as they both "grow" out of my head, often without much conscious awareness on my part. When I've dreamed of having wildly curly hair, I've taken that to suggest unconventional thoughts for me, since my hair in waking life is straight. I once dreamed that I was being hunted as a witch and when I looked in the mirror, I had red hair, instead of the mousy brown hair that I had in waking life at the time of the dream. This dream had the feeling of some past-life energy or experience at play in my life at the time. So when the dreamer notices his or her hair is different than waking life, that can be a useful thing to explore. How we wear our hair is also one of the ways we define ourselves. Like clothing, hairstyles tell the world about us, whether or not what we convey is an accurate representation of our inner selves. So it's worth noticing the hairstyle in the dream and whatever associations arise from that.

When hair stands on end in waking life, it generally means that there's a lot of electricity in the air and lightning is likely. As a symbol, this might mean the imminence of inspiration or spiritual awakening. (In waking life it means "Get off the mountain!" or "Get out of the water!")

If I dream I've shaved my head or cut my hair very short, it suggests to me a ritual cleansing of old thoughts, as novice monks and new recruits into the armed services have their hair cut short. Symbolically, this suggests I've given up on old ways of thinking and am taking on a new set of beliefs and behaviors. If I am bald in a dream, it could represent a more natural change of letting go of old beliefs but not accepting a new structure imposed from outside. I also associate baldness with chemotherapy, so in a dream this could carry the association of needing to cleanse my behavior of something that is metaphorically cancerous.

Body hair, for me, represents my animal nature, generally less groomed and tended than the hair on my head. If body hair in the dream is excessively long or thick, it may represent instinctual energies associated with that part of the body.

"Hay Bale Structure"

A friend told me the following dream:

I'm in my house and I look out and see a structure made of bales of hay, round at the base and conical but unfinished. The bales are far enough apart at the bottom that someone could wriggle through the space between them. There's a man taking a picture of it, and I run out, very upset.

Two images came to mind almost immediately. The first, an Irish stacked-slate house, a sacred space or hermit house, stacked without mortar in such a sturdy way that no rain has come in during the hundreds of years it's been standing. The second image/association comes from the fable of the three pigs: the house made of straw. A structure made of widely spaced hay bales will prove impermanent, and is already open to the weather.

Since my friend is in the early public stages of her career, in my version of the dream I can't help but project that this new career I'm building feels as tenuous as this hay bale structure, with plenty of wiggle room. In my version of the dream, I'm upset that the photographer is recording this in its incomplete and fragile state.

On the other hand, I know hay bales can be used to build very sturdy and efficient homes when covered with adobe, so maybe I'm storing the bales for a future project that I don't want to make public just yet.

I've used hay in my garden as mulch, so following that association, the upset I feel would be about my public life (recordable by anyone with a camera) intruding on my truly private time, which in this case would be gardening. And gardening itself would represent a grounded, authentic life, one in which I'm unafraid to get my hands dirty and spend time in meditation with the physical world.

When the dreamer told the dream, she Spoonerized "bales of hay" and said "bays of hale" (or "bays of hail") which could be an indication of strength and good health, or "Cries of 'Hail'" and therefore a warning of some danger. Either way, attention to the health of my body and the health of my garden is called for.

Horse

Horses are associated both with the sun in that they pull the chariots of sun gods, and with the moon in that they are seen in ocean waves which are subject to tides. They denote power and strength, as well as freedom. Because they can learn to communicate with humans (especially humans who attempt to understand them), in a dream they can represent enormous power available to our control. The horse enabled long-distance travel before the advent of modern transportation, and so is associated with travel and journeys. We still measure engine power according to "horse power," and so a horse in a dream is a symbol of both a standard of measure and an antiquated way of thinking still in use.

When I dream of riding horses I have similar associations to bicycle dreams, in that there's a certain balance and elegance to the mode of transportation. With horses, however, there's also the fact that the steed is sentient and has its own wisdom.

Our expression "get back on the horse" means to attempt something difficult after failing at it previously. In that sense, the horse is an unpredictable challenge that might throw the rider to the ground or carry her where she wants to go.

Horses can be associated with demonic energy, as in the Four Horsemen of the Apocalypse, or the horse sculpture at Denver International Airport which killed its creator.[14] Yet they can also be gentle and sweet. The paradoxical associations show how deeply ingrained in our collective psyche the image of the horse is.

House

I dream often of houses, sometimes houses I recognize from waking life, sometimes ones created fully from my imagination, and often a hybrid of the two. When I dream of my childhood home I always look to see if the dream is speaking to some belief or issue I've held since those very young days. When my oldest daughter was getting ready to leave for college, I dreamed frequently of the first house my husband and I bought together, where we lived when we were first married. I understood that it stood as a symbol of our shifting relationship as we entered into a new phase in our lives, just as we adjusted to living together when we were newlyweds.

Often I dream a variation on the theme of discovering rooms in my house that I never knew existed. I know many people share these dreams, though the specifics vary greatly. One of my friends reported that the rooms she discovers are full of art supplies and she realizes she can participate in her artistic endeavors there. When I discover unknown spaces, they are usually large empty rooms and

---

[14] http://www.denverpost.com/ci_8961169

my thought is "I could store so much stuff here!" I know this resonates with my waking life experience of having boxes and boxes of family archives that I don't really have room for, and my longing for a space to store them that wouldn't impinge on my family's spaces. But since it's a dream symbol, I would be stopping short of potential understanding if I stopped at the obvious meaning.

Unexpected, unknown rooms in houses tend to be about the dreamer's untapped potential. In the case of my friend, the dreams come with the reminder that there is the potential for creativity and artistic expression even amid the important daily duties that absorb time. In my dreams, I think the dreams come to remind me that there's enough room in the world for my work. I make the association between "storage" and "stories," so I think I'm not always recognizing the potential of the stories I have to tell.

Houses can also represent our bodies. I've seen amazing work in dream circles when someone draws the floor plan of the house in his or her dream and we read the drawing as a human body. Often the main action of the dream shows where in the body there's a problem. The action in the dream often sheds light on the underlying nature of the problem.

Laughter and Crying

I had a dream in which I wept in one section, and laughed big belly laughs in the next. I've had both of these experiences in other dreams many times in my life, but I don't recall another dream that featured both. They are apparently opposite emotions, but are actually separated by a very thin veil, in my experience.

When I was first trying to understand my dreams, probably in my teen years, I read somewhere that emotion in dreams came to balance out the apparent opposite emotion in waking life. So if I'd been blue for a long time and I dreamed of laughter, it would lighten my mood. And if I wept in dreams, it signified that I'd neglected some burden in my waking life, like some giant scale that had to be balanced.

I no longer understand laughing and crying in dreams as literal balancing, though I've certainly experienced emotional relief from expressing my feelings in my dream. I've thought a lot about Jeremy Taylor's projection that laughter, especially, but also tears, are markers of surprise in a dream, a place where some new understanding has awoken. In waking life, we laugh at the punch line of a good joke, when we've been led to expect one thing and suddenly another viewpoint is presented that also fits the story but was utterly unexpected. Tears can mark surprise as well: When an understanding I may have had at some shallow level suddenly rests in my body, and when that understanding carries grief, then tears find their way into my dreams.

Sometimes, I wake up laughing. Sometimes the dream still strikes me as funny, but often I don't see the humor in it. These dreams usually have images that I have to work a little harder to understand, since they come from the very edge of my conscious awareness. One of my dream sisters said that laughter in dreams for her is a moment of enlightenment, which makes a lot of sense to me, since enlightenment is bound to be surprising.

Lighthouse

As a symbol, the lighthouse has a lot of power. It serves as a beacon for ships at sea, showing the edge of the land. If the sea is a symbol for the vast unconscious, the lighthouse serves to mark the boundary of conscious thought. For me, this is a symbol with deeply personal meaning, as I associate it with the shining of unconditional love of family—in that my sister is fond of lighthouses and my mom grew up near the sea. So I associate lighthouses with the two women who watched over me growing up and have always accepted me. A lighthouse also appeared for me in a hypnotic state when I was guided to discover my own potential. I had to bring light from a star and put it in a lighthouse for all to see. I interpreted the image as essentially saying I shouldn't hide my light under a bushel. Let's all reclaim our light and let it shine in the world, so that those sailing in the waters of the unconscious can find their way to shore.

Marriage

Getting married in dreams is symbolic of a union of two parts of myself. If I dream I'm marrying someone I don't know, it might be that there's a part of me I'm so unfamiliar with that I don't even recognize it as part of myself. Or I might be marrying someone I do recognize, but would rather not marry. In that case, it suggests to me that my dream wants me to withdraw some projections from that person and integrate them more fully into the wholeness of my being. Generally, marriage in a dream is a good sign, suggesting that I've done some inner work of integration. Of course, much depends on the context of my waking life. If I'm in the midst of planning my wedding in waking life, a marriage dream might come to help me understand whether or not I'm making the right choice, or to alert me to possible problems that I need to be aware of as I move forward. If I'm already married in waking life and dream of marrying my current partner, this could mean that I am withdrawing projections from my partner, or that a renewal of vows might be a good idea. If I'm single in waking life, the dream is most likely about consciously integrating my own psyche.

Mirrors

I've often heard Jeremy Taylor refer to dreams as "the magic mirror that never lies." Dreams, if we can unpack them, reflect us back to ourselves. And what I see in a mirror in a dream is often a glimpse of my truest self. I'd like to talk about two mirrors—one in a dream I had the good fortune to offer my dream group, and the other in waking life.

The first mirror was a mirror in a bathroom, the room in the house where I am, potentially, most honest with myself, at least about my body. I'm the observer in the dream, and the action unfolds before me like a movie that I have no influence over. I glimpse the reflection of one of the dream actresses as she looks into a mirror at the back of a bathroom stall. There are tears in her eyes, and I think that this was an interesting choice by the director to show the audience how she's feeling. A moment later she comes out of the bathroom determined to take action.

The mirror is quite distant from me, the observer, and yet I see the woman's tears clearly. I can't tell you too much about how she looked otherwise, so clearly the tears are central. I interpret that in the dream as sadness about the inevitable transformation that will result from her action, yet that sadness does nothing to stop her from her chosen path. So there's a grief piece, and when I look deepest into my heart, I find grief there, but also her determination to change the things that create the grief.

The other mirror was a waking life moment, when my dad was helping me out of a tight spot (I forgot to bring my charge cable for my Nissan Leaf) and we had to take two cars across town so I could leave mine charging at the dealership while we had our visit. On the way to the dealership, I got out ahead of him in traffic. I stopped at a light and the road in my rear view mirror was empty pretty much as far back as I could see. The light didn't change, and didn't change, and pretty soon, the rear view window showed his car emerging from the distance. The light didn't change. He pulled in behind me, and I waved, watching him in the mirror. He waved back, mildly amused, acknowledging me on this tandem journey.

When I "read" this as a dream, I remember that things behind me in dreams often represent shadow—not necessarily dark shadow or bright shadow, but the things that remain unconscious to me and have an effect on how I behave. And the mirror shows me a part of myself that is true. I see in that mirror the first target of my projections about what the mature masculine looks like. He's loyal and good-natured, happy to be of help when help is needed, able to go along with sudden changes in plans. He has a strong streak of practicality—just do what needs doing and don't fuss about it. In my dream, I see these qualities in his reflection in the mirror, so they are deep and intrinsic parts of myself which I don't generally consciously acknowledge, but which I appreciate very much in my dad.

"Missing Finger"

While studying the fairy tale "The Handless Maiden," I had this dream.

In a building, I can't find my car key. Somehow I realize it's in my shoe.

I'm trapped in a game of Cocoman, my friend S. is one of the people running it. I'm looking for a way to escape. On the street I see a dad trying to comfort his child, who's crying at a creepy ghost-like sound. A small cart like a grocery cart comes through the crowd on the street. It's full of peaches and some peels. I go out and tell the man with the cart that the food processor bowl in his cart is mine. I dump grape seeds and skins by the grape vine in the divider of the road. I tell the man to take the cart and forget he ever saw me.

At one point, I find my missing finger (middle or ring finger of the left hand). The finger I find is black like an overcooked hot dog and I doubt I'll be able to reattach it, but I put it back on and later (when helping the peach cart guy), I look down at my hand and my finger is reattaching well, still discolored, but healthier.

When I woke, I couldn't remember which finger it had been, because I could remember it equally well both ways. This isn't uncommon in dreams, and suggests that both scenarios apply—I can work the dream with either image, and ultimately with both. It's only my linear, waking mind that needs to have it be one or the other. The dreaming mind is comfortable with it being either/both.

If it's my second finger, it's the finger of flipping the bird at someone. This would suggest anger, standing up for myself, and a defiant energy that is unafraid. In my waking life, it's not a gesture I use, nor an energy I've claimed as my own very often. I preferred a peace-keeping role to a standing-up-for-myself role, which would explain why the finger was missing and blackened from being disconnected. Yet the dream suggests that I have the ability to re-integrate that energy into my behavior.

If it's my third finger, it's where I wear my wedding ring, and so is a sign of commitment. The fact that it's been missing would suggest a lack of commitment until now to the task at hand. Perhaps this is a spiritual task, with the grapes' seeds and skins suggesting the left-over matter from juicing the grapes. I'm returning this material to nurture the grape vine so that it can grow more grapes in the future. All of this suggests that maybe I've been preparing to make wine (often associated with religious ritual), and I in my act of composting, I participate in a practical and spiritual approach to nurturing the plants that sustain me.

Whatever the commitment the dream refers to, if I think of both fingers together, I think about how sometimes I have to assume a rather defiant attitude toward the demands of the world if I want to protect my commitment to my creative work. The middle finger serves as guardian to the commitment of the ring finger.

Naked in Public

Dreams of being naked in public places are, for me, about revealing more of my true self to the world. If no one around me even notices that I'm naked, or partially dressed, the dream is telling me that I can safely show the world more of who I am. Naked dreams can also be about a feeling that I've felt more exposed than I'm generally comfortable with, and if no one in the dream seems to care, my dream is telling me that whatever I imagine, others around me aren't noticing as much as I think they are.

Being naked is also suggestive of innocence—we enter the world naked without the socially imposed restrictions of needing to cover ourselves. So a dream of being naked in public might be a reminder of my innocence in a particular situation.

Night Sky

I've learned to pay attention to the quality of light in dreams as a clue to how conscious the problem or situation is that the dream illustrates. If the dream takes place in full daylight, it's likely to be about a situation I'm familiar with. If the dream plays out in the dark, it's likely that the meanings of the dream are ones that are newly arising in my consciousness.

When I was expecting my first child, I had a dream that Kwan Yin appeared to me in the night. We stood in the backyard of my childhood home, gazing up at the night sky, full of stars and constellations I'd never seen in waking life but which were familiar to my dreaming self. She told me that I could have chosen to remain there, in the heavens, but I'd chosen to live during this time, when even the prey had become predators. I saw a deer attacking something in illustration.

The dream had other elements, and though it was a "big" dream in terms of emotional impact, I've never found it written down in any of my journals. (I kept my dream journal more sporadically then.) But I've thought about the dream often, especially of the night sky, so vivid in the dream, and its association with "Heaven." The suggestion in the dream, that I could have stayed there, among the stars, I've always understood to mean that if my soul had chosen, I could have remained disincarnate, in the heavens.

For me, there's an association with being part of something larger than myself when I think of Heaven. It's a place of love, of returning to the great ocean of spirit, that part of me that often remains largely unconscious. This is true for other dreamers as well, as Jeremy Taylor notes in *The Living Labyrinth: Exploring Universal Themes in Myths, Dreams, and the Symbolism of Waking Life*. "Dreams in which the archetypal energies of the collective unconscious make themselves known often use ... imagery evocative of the "fathomless ocean," the "infinite sky," "angels" (and/or "demons"), "ancient lost continents and civilizations" and so forth."[15]

It is the very depth of the night sky, the impossible distance between the stars that look so near to one another, that evokes a sense of the divine. The incomprehensibility of it stands as a metaphor for the Divine, God, All That Is, the Unnameable.

Constellations are a wonderful example of how we use projection and pattern seeking. Cultures all over the world see patterns in the stars and assign mythological meanings and stories to those patterns. So in that sense, seeing constellations in my dream would invite me to look at the ways I assign meaning and seek relationships between things that might not be near one another at

---

[15] Taylor, *The Living Labyrinth*, p. 57.

all. Seeking relationships between disparate elements in my life is a form of creativity, so seeing the night sky in my dream carries all of those connotations.

Ocean

There may be nothing more archetypal than the ocean. As humans, we've depended on its waters to provide food and entertainment (sailing, surfing), and we've suffered when its enormous power has risen up in unexpected ways. Tsunamis and storms remind us that we have not truly mastered natural forces.

In dreams, the ocean often represents the unconscious, but it can also be a great well of emotion. When dreamers have reported dreams of struggling underwater, there is usually, at least at one level, a place in their lives where emotions have overwhelmed them. By contrast, dreaming of breathing under water suggests the ability to survive the great overwhelm of emotion.

I've dreamed of the ocean and its creatures many times. In waking life, I love walking along beaches and finding the treasures tossed up by the waves, with the sound of the surf helping me relax. I sense eternity when I watch the waves rolling in, and find comfort in the fact that my life, no matter how difficult at the time, is but a heartbeat in the life of the world. But in my dreams, the ocean comes to remind me that I need to be quick on my feet to dodge the tsunamis that life throws my way. Or that my little boat won't protect me from the life I'm destined to experience. Or that I am not really so very different from the creatures that live in the water's depths.

Where the ocean meets the shore is an interesting space in dreams, evoking the place where unconscious thoughts lap against consciousness. If the waves in the dreams are large, the shore could represent the place I am safe from uncontrolled emotion, or perhaps, if I'm in the water, the place I'm trying to reach.

(See also the discussion of my tsunami dream in the "Signs and Portents" section.)

"The Other Wife with a Missing Right Arm"

I once opened my dream journal at random and the first symbol I noticed was "the other wife" with a missing right arm. Here's the reading I did of that symbol for my blog:

There are a lot of directions to go with this. I'll start with the wife. She's not the waking life wife of the character in the dream, so she must be his other wife. I see in that an alternate understanding of my role as wife, of the feminine that I see as "other," as different from myself.

In the dream, the husband is sad because his other wife used to be a writer, and now her right (write) arm is gone, however she's living off royalties from earlier work. This dream came at a time when writing time was carefully carved out of a life suddenly taken over by Life Events which demanded my attention. So the symbol of the missing writing arm is fairly obvious at that level. What levels am I not seeing so easily? When I ask myself that question, I think of "righting wrongs" and my prayer that my work may do its bit to heal wounds, lift tired spirits, and remind people of beauty during hard times. That too, had felt missing in the few weeks previous to finding this dream in my journal, as my world had undergone big changes.

Yet in the dream, the wife is living off royalties from previous projects. In my waking life, this is most certainly not the case, at least not literally. In some sense, it must be true metaphorically, or I wouldn't have dreamed this dream. So what are the metaphorical royalties I'm earning from the years of writing practice? Trust in the process comes to mind first. I've learned how to listen for story, and if I prepare to write what I hear, the words will come. This itself could be a metaphor for listening to my own inner guidance about life. So the dream reminds me to listen to my intuition about everything, in the same way I listen to the stories that I write.

Another payoff from my commitment to writing is that it led me to a deeply dedicated tribe of writer friends who share my passion for a good story and understand the sometimes tortuous path of a writing life. And they, in turn, stand in as symbols for all of the networks I've built in the life I've led. These are the people who will keep me grounded, no matter whether I'm flying high on success or slogging through the doldrums. Friendships more precious than gold.

So that part of the dream is enormously reassuring. But the missing arm still piques my curiosity. One of the first phrases that occurred to me when I decided to write about this dream was "I'd give my right arm" followed by "cost an arm and a leg." The former phrase begs the question, what would I give my right arm for? For those of us who are right-handed, this would carry the weight of my work in the world, and my ability to get myself noticed (by raising my hand). What would I give all that for? What would I willingly sacrifice a part of myself for? The second phrase carries the same implication of a thing that costs a great deal, but has less of the willing sacrifice archetype to it, at least in my reading. It's more something that I paid because I had to, for something I really needed.

So this "other" wife carries these shadow pieces of sacrificing her work in the world, of not fulfilling her true calling. I'm reminded to touch in with my inner guidance and see what it is that I need to do to integrate this shadow in pursuit of wholeness, while being reminded that I have great abundance in the metaphorical royalties of my life.

"Packing to Go Home"

Over the last couple of years I've had a recurring theme in my dreams. I'm at a hotel/cabin/conference and am packing to go home. The actual packing of a suitcase is usually the opening for a longer dream, and the scenarios that follow or coincide with my packing vary greatly from dream to dream. I've talked about this image with a couple of trusted dream workers, and the strongest "aha" I got was the idea that I'm not "at home" with whatever my situation currently is, but that I want to bring along what I've learned from being "away" when I do return home. I'm still not certain what part of myself isn't "at home," though there's always been a restlessness in my creative life, so perhaps I haven't yet found my truest avenue of creative expression.

I know that writing saved my sanity, but after years and years of daily practice, it sometimes felt more like a duty than a salvation. Painting takes me to a very satisfying creative space, but the overhead of set up and clean up (and the lack of a good space) makes it less practical for frequent expression. So maybe there's still something out there I haven't encountered that would truly make me feel at home in myself.

Or perhaps this is a metaphor for life itself as a preparation for death. I'm gathering the things that the dream ego identifies with—clothing, primarily, which would be a shallow, outward presentation of persona to the world—in order to bring it with me when I return home/die. In this reading, perhaps the dream suggests that I give too much weight to how the world sees me, and ought instead to be focused on my creative life.

In the dreams, I'm never actually hauling my suitcases to a car or bus or airplane, but am just in the temporary space of the hotel or cabin, gathering my things into a suitcase. If I could get lucid in one of these dreams, perhaps I could better remember what exactly I am packing, beyond a vague feeling of it being clothes. This is a dream I know I haven't yet fully "unpacked."

"Penguin and Whale"

A friend sent me the following dream:

I was in and out of the water all night - don't know why, and I wasn't fighting it. Swimming and/or boating as I remember. At one point I had to leave to go do something, and when I came back the water had a thin layer of ice on it. I remember thinking that this was strange because it wasn't cold out. I looked across the water and I saw fins break the surface of the ice. Kind of looked like sharks, but I knew them to be whales - maybe Orcas. Not menacing - just there. Then - and here's the weird part, I looked close to shore and saw penguins swimming under the water. One of them looked at me, (and now it gets REALLY weird), and took on sort of a "human" persona - a small child - but still a penguin - kind of said, "goodbye" to me, (no idea how, but he did), and then in a real excited fashion took off to join his friends. I was fine with it. I almost joined him, but watched him swim off.

Then my friend asked if the penguin represented one of his children, a young teenager.

I sent the following response with my projections:

For me, the water is both the unconscious and emotion, and the crust of ice is a barrier I've erected to not experience my unconscious/emotional life fully. I do this because it's overwhelming to get into it fully, so it's a protective maneuver for me. The whales are a loaded symbol. For me, they're always (at one level at least) about my true calling in the world. Like Jonah in the whale, he's brought through a dark time to the very place God wanted him to be, even though he tried to avoid the call. The lesson here is that we don't have a lot of choice about what we're called to do in this life. We're going to end up there one way or another.

The penguin/child is fascinating. Male Emperor penguins hold their eggs on their feet to protect them from the ice for two months, so I see a lot of nurturing energy in this. The question you had at the end about the penguin being your child is intriguing— remembering that everything in the dream is "me" but is also multi-layered symbology, I have to say that in my dream the penguin saying goodbye could be a symbol of my child growing up (the teen years are all about differentiation from the parents), but could also be about some part of myself that I'm parenting. Penguins are also symbolic of growing dream awareness, because they move so well in the ocean/unconscious. In my dream, the penguin's enthusiasm is an invitation to join him, which I don't do, maybe because the whales (my calling) are still a bit off-shore and I'm just beginning to get glimpses of them so I'm not quite ready to plunge into the water. But I know, in the dream, that it's okay that the penguin is happy there.

So my projection is that this dream invites me even deeper into the unconscious, into dreams, into nurturing (myself and my kids), and into emotion. For me, the dream evokes an invitation to pursue what's really interesting.

(See also "Whales")

Pigs

I dreamed of two young pigs. One was mostly black, the other mostly pink, and they were about two feet long. I'm first struck by the fact that there were two of them, since "twins" or doubles in dreams often represent something new coming into conscious awareness. This is reinforced by the fact that they were two feet long.

Pigs are complex symbols. They're associated linguistically with gluttony, and are associated often with dirt and filth. Yet in the dream, they are more like pets, snuggling together on a bed taking a nap, so the gluttony and filth don't create much of an "aha" for me. Yet they are also highly intelligent animals, one of the most intelligent that we humans regularly raise for food. So they offer the complexity of being a symbol of intelligence, but also potential food sources, which in a dream would symbolize non-physical nourishment. In my dream they are also pets, and so represent unconditional love. Archetypally, pigs are associated with abundance, growing from two-pound babies to 300-400 pound adults. The pigs in my dream are young, so perhaps represent abundance that isn't yet in its fullness.

President Obama

In September of 2012 I had two dreams about President Barack Obama. In one I'm wheeling a hand truck or dolly across a campus and remember seeing Obama wheeling it when he brought it over to me, and Michelle and their daughters were with him. In the other, he sits on the floor beside me in a crowded cafeteria to eat with me, and brings me a glass of water before posing for pictures with a young girl.

In an election season, it's not too surprising that I would dream of political figures, but I don't recall ever dreaming of an American president other than Obama. I've had other dreams of him over the years, usually involving brief meetings and rather ordinary circumstances. In addition to the fact that our values line up fairly well, I expect I feel some affinity for him because we are close in age, and it meant a lot to me to have a president who grew up in the same years I did, watching the same TV shows, being the same age when big events happened in the world.

But of course, the Barack Obama who shows up in my dreams is not the real man, whom I've never met. The fact that we've never met and yet he's been so much in the spotlight makes it easy to project on him. As a symbolic figure, I see him as an integration of bright and dark shadow. Jeremy Taylor has done an excellent job of pointing out the mistaken literalism at play in racist attitudes in a blog post for Psychology Today.[16] However, I don't think you need to understand a lot of theory to see how people with darker skin in our culture have had negative projections thrust upon them by people with lighter skin. When Obama was elected, he became a lightning rod for all the unconscious fears of people who still see their own shadows in other people.

At the same time, Obama carried the bright shadow projection of millions of Americans. Some of us wept with joy that our country had grown up enough to elect someone other than a pale male to the highest office in the land, and we saw in Obama the possibility of diplomacy rather than war, of compassion instead of greed. We saw in him intelligence, a man of lofty ideals grounded in a solid marriage, parenthood, and an unprivileged background. We longed, as he suggested, to bend the arc of history.

Neither of these sets of projections are President Obama, so when he shows up in my dream the figure carries all these projections, both my own personal ones and those of the larger culture. In that sense (and in his parentage) he stands as a symbol for the integration of light and dark. For me, that suggests that when I dream of him, I am meeting that part of myself that has successfully integrated the qualities in myself that I see as good with those I see as bad. He also represents ambition, success, finding strength in family, and compassion. And hard work, when he's wheeling a hand truck.

---

[16] http://www.psychologytoday.com/blog/the-wisdom-your-dreams/201010/dreaming-racism-and-the-unconscious

Finally, when politicians show up in my dream, I always wonder how much more functional our government would be if dream work were a regular part of politicians' lives. I'd love to see the arc of history bend that direction!

"Pursued Through Cinderblock Corridors"

Starting when I was very young, maybe three years old, I had a recurring nightmare:

I'm running away from someone who intends to hurt me if he catches me. The walls of the hallway I'm in are cinder block, the corridors straight but laid out in a maze. I run, too terrified, too aware of the menacing presence behind me to look back. I'm running for my life. I turn a corner. I'm in a locker room, a swimming pool locker room. Trapped.

At this point I'd wake in the full grip of nightmare energy—alarm, adrenaline, and sobbing terror. The details could change in subtle ways, but the constants of the dream were the terror, the pursuit, and the labyrinth of short, straight hallways. And underlying it, the persistent impression that the halls led to a locker room, though sometimes I woke before I got there.

I had the dream into my teens. I have wondered what might have happened in a locker room at a young age, but I have no conscious memory of abuse in a locker room, other than the negative association with swimming lessons. I hated the cold water, the sensation of water on my face, and the chill of evaporating moisture when I got out onto dry land again. Although I didn't, as an adult, experience the nightmare again in a dream state, the imagery still haunts me.

The shadow figure in the dream, a man wanting to change me, remained unseen until I practiced dream re-entry with the dream. He was always behind, which I associate with unconscious. By the time I tried re-entering the dream, I'd had a little practice in life in turning to face my fears, both in waking life and in dreams. I was away at Billie Ortiz's Dream Retreat, and had time for a rest. I went to my room, lay on the bed, and closed my eyes to fully imagine the dream. And to shape it.

It takes less than eye-blink to stand (in my imagination) in the cinder block hall. I remember the panic, rather than fully experience it. I turn to face my pursuer. I experience the imagined dream from the dual perspective of my adult self and my small, three-year-old self. The man is an adult, so from my dual perspective, he is my height/very tall. His features vague, I think he's not old, but not young. With both hands, he holds out a ball of light, a bit too big for his fingertips to touch each other. He communicates, "I've brought your authentic self back to you."

I can't remember now if I snapped out of the imagined dream then, or if I took the offered light. Writing this, I imagine that I do take the light into my hands, and I see the many ways I've been reclaiming my authentic self ever since I turned to face that most ancient, primal, and important fear that pursued me through my youth. I'm sure the recurring dreams carries other meanings too—the expression of panic at the inevitability of growing up, for example, which is one reason why it faded as I did grow up in waking life.

The re-imagining of confronting the fear, of meeting an adult masculine aspect of myself and hearing with the adult/child feminine part, is an evolving experience. I try to remember the message: "Here, reclaim your light." It is, for me, an exquisite example of the archetypal Shadow holding hostage the exact gift I need to grow and evolve. I take the light in my hands, and hold it to my heart. It enters my heart, spreading outward to fill my body and, I hope, cast some light on my journey.

Red

According to Jeremy Taylor, when people report they dream only in black and white, and then they start dreaming in color, the first color they usually dream is red.[17] This is generally because colors are often associated with emotions, and the strongest emotion is often anger. In our society, boys usually get the message that anger is the only socially acceptable emotion for them to display, while for girls, anger is often the least acceptable emotion. So anger stands in, especially in men's dreams, for all the other emotions. Red and anger go together in our lexicon, when we say someone is "seeing red." The bullfighter's cape is designed to excite a bull to anger, and even though the motion of the cloth probably matters

---

[17] Taylor, *Dream Work*, p. 29.

more to the bull than the color, we humans play out an archetypal association by using a red cape.

Red can also represent blood. One of the first associations that always arises for me is of bloodlines, family connections, ancestors and descendants. For women this association is perhaps even more embodied than for men, since women get monthly reminders of how closely blood is connected to reproduction.

Besides anger, red can connote passion and love (again associated with blood) or even intoxication (red, red wine). Depending on the dreamer's experience, red might evoke feelings of guilt and shame. It can symbolize guilt because of the blood spilled in murder. We blush when we're embarrassed, and so are "red-faced" or we can be caught "red-handed." Red ink or pencil is frequently used to correct written work, and being "in the red" means being in debt.

Red gets our attention, and so we make stop signs and stop lights red. In many cities, fire trucks are red. So red in a dream could suggest the need to stop, or the emergent need for action. Many nations use red on their flags, evoking the courage and sacrifice of soldiers who shed their blood for their country. Lately I've also been trying to cut my way through government red tape. These ways that we use red for the safety of the community, or to symbolize our patriotic spirit, or to talk about our experience of labyrinthine government procedures, all lead back to a sense of being part of a greater tribe.

Sand

See "Time and Clocks"

Seeds

A friend told me a dream in which the last image was a decorative pin the dreamer had made with seed beads sewn onto leather. Because of the work we'd done on earlier parts of the dream, she had the realization that the seeds were the experiences she'd had in life, that everything she'd known was metaphorically sewn to her skin. Out of the seeds grows beauty. Some of the ways I project beauty onto the dreamer of this dream are in her great wisdom, and her ability to live her life with an open heart, despite the profound endurance she's shown in grueling circumstances. The images of those seed beads stayed with me.

A couple of weeks later, I had a dream that opened with this scene:

I'm talking with someone about casting seeds—the other person says I should cast my seeds far and wide so the one person who needs that seed will get it. I am moved, recognizing I need and have received such metaphorical seeds from others. I am with other people who have had no luck getting the seeds out of the pods. I put the pods in a cup of water and shake the pods. The seeds start coming out and into the cup and I am weeping as I fling them, moved by the idea that they'll go and one may find its home, and moved also by gratitude for others who have gone before and cast seeds that I have found when I needed them. I'm flinging them over my front garden. I fling a handful of dirt at the end.

The final image of the dream was: *I notice my right hand is stained woad blue, irregular and dull, with some dark patches, unevenly stained like I've been processing grapes.*

At the time of the dream, I was working on publicity for an upcoming workshop. I immediately saw the seeds in the dream as the various announcements I'd been putting out into the world. The dream convinced me to go ahead with it, even though I had only one person signed up at that point. I ended up with nine people at the workshop, a perfect size and a delightful group of people who were drawn to play in, and with, their creativity. We had a wonderful time and several people produced work that surprised them.

Of course, seeds can represent many things; the seed of an idea, the literal seed of a plant, the seed of new animal life. In my dream, I see most clearly the meaning of offering my teaching to the world, but I don't limit that understanding to my workshops. Teaching is simply sharing what I know, in any way I can. I hope that this book reaches those who need it, and I hope my fiction writing touches readers who will find in my stories some "aha" moments of understanding themselves.

When I write fiction, the sensation is one of listening for the story, of showing up at the keyboard or notebook and allowing the story to flow through me. By showing up every day, I've developed the ability to jump into the story where I left off, even if I'm interrupted frequently during my work time. Just like people who begin to keep dream journals often discover that their dreams become more vivid and memorable, I have found that by offering my attention to the stories, the stories respond by coming through more easily. I hadn't been thinking about that with the woad-blue hand, but when I worked the dream with a friend, he projected the association of woad with Celtic warriors, who, in his words, "Just had to show up for the battle to be won." As I thought about that, I remembered what I know and often forget—that the true work is the showing up, and I should cast my work widely and let the seeds fall where they may. I might never know who will find them useful, but I owe it to the world to cast them.

Shoes, Socks, and Bare Feet

One of the associations that always rings a bell for me when footwear or bare feet appear in my dreams is that this is about my spiritual path. Shoes, in this case, would be the accepted, possibly inherited religious/spiritual beliefs I hold, or those I was raised with. Socks would be an intermediate phase, a kind of transition, and bare feet would be walking my own authentic spiritual path.

These aren't the only associations, however. I've had dreams of losing one of my shoes—in particular a clog-style shoe, which brings up the idea that whatever has been clogging up my journey is on its way out. I have a friend who dreamed frequently about buying fancy shoes in various colors with various decorations on them, and when we dug into her associations with shoes like that, it turned out they were the kind her sister usually wore and the dreams were showing her places where she wanted to emulate her sister's successful lifestyle, even though she didn't consciously respect that lifestyle.

Bare feet can also be a sign of a more natural approach to living in the world and being "grounded" by walking with skin touching earth. If I'm barefoot in a restaurant, though, it might be a sign of disregarding regulations and rules imposed by establishments. And, of course, if I had a "barefoot and pregnant and in the kitchen" dream, I'd want to look at how extensively my idea of my self-worth and role in life was formed by outdated sexist attitudes about a woman's place in the world. If I dream of walking in someone else's shoes, it might be a sign of my growing compassion.

Snakes

Traditionally, snakes are a very complicated symbol, being both male (obviously phallic) and female (flexible and fluid in movement). They also symbolize transformation and growth, with the shedding of skin, and healing, as they are present even today in the physician's traditional symbol. For me, having grown up in the west, rattlesnakes represent the most prevalent poisonous snake of my childhood, a thing to be wary of when out moving through the world, but not paralyzed by terror about. They do, after all, generally give warning, which not all snakes do. They represent a wild element, but almost a backyard sort of wildness, not completely exotic.

In the Old Testament, the snake is the agent of the devil, tempting Eve into tasting the fruit of the Tree of Knowledge, leading to Adam and Eve's exile from the Garden of Eden. So in a dream, a snake might represent this temptation to learn things that I'm not really ready for, or to evolve in consciousness to the point where I can no longer be "innocent" or blissfully ignorant of the evils in the world.

Spaceships

While this isn't a symbol that's shown up in my own dreams, I've heard it from a lot of people and have worked with this symbol in groups. Carl Jung argued that flying saucers in dreams were a kind of mandala seen from the side, offering the symbolic idea that if we could communicate with the alien intelligence that created these space ships, our problems would be solved.[18] For me, spaceships represent our hopes and fears as a species that we are not alone in the universe, and that there is some superior intelligence at work. Because spaceships are flown by aliens, they can represent the vehicles for new understanding coming into awareness—getting a glimpse of an "alien" idea.

---

[18] Jung, *Flying Saucers*, pp. 20-21.

Spiral

Any time a spiral shows up in a dream, it carries with it the resonance of all spirals. In *An Illustrated Encyclopaedia of Traditional Symbols*, J. C. Cooper writes: *"The spiral is symbolized by all that is helical: snail shells, sea shells, the ear, the tentacles of the octopus, animal horns, animals like the dog and cat that curl up, the coiled serpent, plants which grow in spiral form such as ivy, fir cones and the unfolding fronds of ferns. It is also associated with ears of gods and kings and with rain-bearing animals and reptiles and with the coiled and sleeping serpent Kundalini."*[19] I agree with all the associations (though I'm not sure what a "rain-bearing animal" is) but I would add the spiral symbolizes all those things as well as being symbolized by them.

Spirals show up in the art of cultures all over the world. Why is the symbol so prevalent? Probably because it is found so widely in nature, in whirlpools and plants, galaxies and DNA. When such an ancient and archetypal symbol appears in a dream, it carries with it the potential that all of the associations will shed light on the meaning of the dream. If I dream of a whirlpool, for example, the spiral shape evokes both galaxies and embryos, and so the import of the dream has a collective level as well as a deeply personal one. It could refer to my ongoing growth of self-awareness with an

---

[19] Cooper, *An Illustrated Encyclopaedia of Traditional Symbols*, p. 157.

emphasis, because of the inward movement of a whirlpool, on the inward focus of that self-awareness.

Before reading Cooper's piece on the spiral, I hadn't made the association with the human ear. A dream with a spiral, then, would emphasize listening, whether to the inner voice or the teachings available in the world. How important the association is would depend on the context of the dream, of course, but it would be worth asking the dreamer if such an association elicits any "aha" of understanding.

Like the snake, the spiral represents "an archetypal path of growth, transformation and psychological or spiritual journey."[20] As we grow in life, we climb the spiral path of understanding, and so to dream of a spiral seashell would carry this meaning, as would dreaming of bindweed. The beauty of dream symbols is that they hold multiple meanings at once, and these archetypal meanings are present even if we're not consciously aware of them. To dream of a spiral is to dream of the cosmos and of the structure of life itself.

Suicide

See "Death"

---

[20] *Book of Symbols,* p. 718.

Teeth

I've often heard people reference the "biting off more than I can chew" phrase when teeth come up as a dream symbol. But I also associate teeth falling out with growing out of childhood—marking a definitive change that I have no control over. So as a metaphor, for me, teeth falling out would suggest I'm going through some growth period that I can't control and maybe don't really want to go through, but it's inevitable. I can try to manage it, but the only way to control it is to keep my mouth shut—which means not expressing myself and not taking in any nourishment, neither of which is a viable option. I've frequently had dreams of molars and crowns falling out, and in waking life I had a horrible problem with a molar shortly after experiencing a profound grief. That same tooth pained me years later during another grief period. So a very personal association for me is that molars in dreams are associated with grief, but that may not be true for others.

Theaters and Auditoriums

A recurring motif in my dreamscape is that I'm trying to find a seat in a theater or outdoor auditorium. Often the only ones available are facing away from the stage, or are behind pillars. Sometimes the dream includes the performance, but usually it's just one of those frustrating dreams of trying to obtain the unobtainable.

Whether the performance is musical or theatrical, it speaks in the language of metaphor, so for me the theater/auditorium is a place where I come to watch metaphor in action. In this way, it's a place of higher levels of thought and awareness than I usually bring to my waking life. The fact that I can't find a seat with a decent view suggests that I still have internal blocks to a full understanding of what's about to unfold.

The performance of a play in a dream serves to remind me that life is a kind of play, or as Shakespeare put it, "All the world's a stage, And all the men and women merely players." As one who has a tendency to take life much too seriously, it is always valuable to be reminded of this perspective.

As an audience member in my dream, I am preparing to receive information, rather than to offer it, a sure sign that I'm still learning, still trying to understand. There's a message, too, in the fact that it's only the dream ego that has a seat facing away from the stage—all the good seats are filled with other aspects of my being that have a better, clearer view of what's going on.

Time and Clocks

I've had and heard many dreams in which time plays a part. Often it takes the form of "I'm supposed to be there/do that/start at a certain time and I realize it's two hours later already." Archetypally, this sort of dream is closely related, in my mind, to the "I'm signed up for a class I didn't know I had and now I have to take a test I know nothing about" dream, and the "I'm onstage with a part in a play I've never heard of/don't know the name of and have no idea what my lines are" dream. All of these dream themes reflect a meta-level in my life, in which hours, tests, and roles I play are all metaphors for how I navigate my life.

When time and clocks show up in dreams, I think about the fact that time is how we measure change. I count the days of my life through the messes that I create and clean up, the meals I eat and digest, the work I give time to, the conversations I have with others, and the passage of the sun. I measure the weeks and months by the changing weather and the cycles of the moon, the years by the growth of my children and the aches and shifting shape of my body. I imagine the passage of decades in the image of a ship's bones gone to rust in the sand. We call some of that change progress, some decline, but we measure our progress and decline through time. So how I dream of time and what I'm trying to do in the dream can give me clues about how I'm doing.

If I'm running late, or it's later than I thought, that might suggest that a part of me would like to be making better progress toward my goals. If I can't read my watch, it might mean that time is not the crucial factor in the situation. If the clock is running backward, I'd have to ask myself if there's some futile hope that I could turn back time, or if I should be retreating to an earlier stage in the project I'm working on. So much depends on the context of the dream.

Finally, sand in a dream always brings up for me "the sands of time." So if I'm trying to climb a sand dune in the dream, my progress or lack thereof would relate to how I'm moving through time, at least at one level. I expect the metaphor arose from the use of hour-glasses, which provide a visual signal for time's passage.

Tornadoes

Throughout history and around the world, people have seen tornadoes as manifestations of God's will. In the Book of Job in the Old Testament, God speaks to Job out of a whirlwind. In Hosea, the whirlwind is the punishment of the wicked. The fearsome power of tornadoes, and wind in general, is associated with the omnipotence of deities. Because of their shape, tornadoes are also associated with spirals and so carry the weight of the created universe, from galaxies to the human ear. Yet a tornado has a wildness to it that suggests vengefulness and fury.

When a tornado shows up in a dream, it often carries with it the metaphorical meaning of a message from the Divine, or our spiritual selves. Jeremy Taylor has a thorough article on tornadoes on his website, and states that in his extensive experience, "The dream 'tornado', over and over again, turns out to be symbol of the dreamer's own personal relationship to the deepest unasked and unanswered psycho-spiritual questions in his/her life, and these issues always have transpersonal implications as well."[21] When I dream of a tornado, then, it's worth asking what questions I've been grappling with, or should be grappling with, in my psyche or spirit.

---

[21] http://www.jeremytaylor.com/dream_work/a_tornado/index.html

We have many images of tornadoes in our collective awareness, from the one in *The Wizard of Oz* to the ones that are caught on video by bystanders, tornado chasers, and news cameras. It's easy to see how such an image could influence a dreamer's nighttime dreams, especially if those images were first seen at an impressionable young age. But it's simplistic to "blame" a movie version of a tornado for repeated tornado dreams. Millions of people have seen *The Wizard of Oz*, yet not every person who saw it for the first time as young child has recurring tornado dreams. A more interesting approach, to me, is to ask why the image captures some people's imaginations so strongly, while not affecting others. My projection is that the tornado shows up in dreams because, as the dreamer, I have a spiritual calling or a deep issue within my psyche that needs my attention. The tornado gets my attention in a big way, especially if the dream feels nightmarish, and by its intensity suggests that the spiritual question is of the utmost importance in my life.

The tornado in *The Wizard of Oz* acts as a transformative agent, taking Dorothy out of her familiar life and depositing her in a strange world where she discovers that she has more power than she'd ever imagined. This symbolism holds true in many tornado dreams, where the new, strange world is a metaphorical one, but the dreamer's ability to discover unexpected abilities and powers is literal.

"Train on the Mountain"

Here's a dream I heard from a friend:

The center is the mountain. It is large, steep, rounded on the top, and devoid of vegetation. On the mountain is a road covered with the train track. The only way around this mountain is to walk the track. I am heading to the other side of the mountain and I must go on this path. I move leftward as I circle the mountain. I worry because I know when the train comes, there will not be room for both of us, the train, and you and I. We are walking together. You seem younger, like an adolescent, and we walk side by side. Our clothes are drab, long, and yet I am totally comfortable. The train is here. We have no room to stand on the side. We do the only thing we can. We hang on to the edge of the road by our fingers, clutching the dirt just inches from the track rail. Our feet dangle in the nothingness below. I am now the observer, watching the train go by as the two hang for their lives. It seems impossible they can hang on for the duration of the train's passing.

Apparently, we make it to the town and on the way back, the train comes once more. This time as I dangle, there is no dirt ledge left, only the rail. I see my fingers wrapped over the top of the rail and I know the train will amputate them and I will surely fall into the darkness below. I am feeling more curious about my lack of options than I feel frightened. I wonder why it couldn't be different, a feeling of resignation.

My response:

For me, the mountain is very breast-like, and so might represent my relationship to feminine, nurturing parts of myself. In my imagined version of the dream, the purpose of the travel is not to get to the town, but the journey itself. The only way around the mountain is to walk along the track, which in my dream is some belief I have about how I should be doing things—a training or lesson, likely one learned in adolescence, as I see my companion as an adolescent. The first time the dream comes, I have the option of just standing on the track, letting this part of me represented by the dream ego die in the impact, but I choose to avoid that and dangle precariously over the abyss instead. The dream allows me to avoid this death the first time, but when I return, the dream offers me another chance to willingly sacrifice who I think I am. This time, I will surely die and lose my fingers in the process. My fingers are very dexterous and sensitive parts of myself, and in losing them I will lose "touch" with this train track, with this old entrained way of doing things.

For me, the part that has to die is the part that sees no other way past my obstacles than this well-laid track that goes around the mountain. I'm resigned rather than frightened because I know, at some level, that this death of who I think I am is necessary before I'll be able to have other options.

Trapeze

I've had some very memorable dreams where I was watching trapeze artists flying over great distances, grasping each other's hands in amazing catches. And then I finally had one where I was on the trapeze myself.

The dream opens with me introducing Jeremy Taylor to an audience. I have a red scarf over my head. I go out, and he has a huge line of people waiting to talk to him. I do a trapeze act with D. W., who preaches as he swings on the trapeze. He says, "Go for a hike, tell someone you love them, forgive someone." At the end, we hug while each on our own trapeze, and then he lets go of the trapeze, curls into a ball, and floats to the ground. I go back inside where Jeremy is. My arms are sore. A woman in the audience asks everyone to give their attention to Jeremy.

Many dream dictionaries don't include "trapeze," though Betty Bethards offers these associations: "High-minded ideas; daring inspiration. Swinging back and forth; indecision."[22] All of these projections elicit "ahas" from me. I swing back and forth between the creative work I do that feels inspired and the work I do in my family that feels more like service. In addition, I project the importance of timing on the symbolic meaning of a trapeze act. I have to be ready to catch my partner when he flies on his own, and I have to know

---

[22] Bethards, *The Dream Book*, p. 157.

when to let go of my own hold on the trapeze bar and trust that I'll be safely caught again.

D.W. is a childhood acquaintance whom I haven't seen in nearly forty years. In that sense, he's a perfect candidate for a dream symbol, since I know nothing of who he is now. What he represents in the dream is based on my projections on him from when we were children. There's innocence about him in my memory and in the dream, and the wisdom that comes from an innocent heart. His advice to exercise, express love, and release old resentments seems a sound prescription for health and wholeness. His gentle descent to the ground suggests that not all landings have to be hard. His curling into a ball suggests a sphere, which is wholeness.

The scene with D.W. and the trapeze is framed with dream work. Jeremy represents that, of course, but also teaching, preaching, and spreading the metaphorical word. So for me this dream is about my calling to write, to explore meaning through metaphor, and to help people understand their dreams and get in touch with their own creativity. The dream reminds me that at the center of that, I need to forgive myself, and take care of myself, and trust the universe to catch me when I take a leap of faith. All easier said than done, but like a trapeze act, it takes practice.

Tree

Talking about trees as a symbol is like talking about birds, in that there are some archetypal associations that every tree shares— The Tree of Life, staying rooted while reaching up, and family trees. From trees we learn metaphorical lessons, like the idea that if we stay flexible, we're more likely to bend than break when life's winds blow through. We live in breathing symbiosis with trees, and we're becoming more aware, as a species, of just how important our co-breathing is. Some among us do their part to bring us back from the brink of habitat destruction by planting trees.

Archetypally, trees are also associated with the Axis Mundi, or the axis of the Earth. In many cultures, a particular genus has this association; the Norse ash tree Yggdrasil being a prime example. The Tree of Life or World Tree in many cultures connects Earth with Heaven. Because forests regenerate when left to their own processes, trees are symbolic of eternal life. I see this as connected to the tree's symbolism of the family tree as well. We have our roots in our ancestors—more literally than we suspected, as the science of epigenetics is now discovering—and our descendants carry human life forward. While an individual life comes and goes, the whole of our connection to past and present life is the metaphorical tree, eternal and immense. I've heard very fruitful dream work around the metaphorical meaning of the family tree when the dream-maker provides this image. Are the branches alive, or cut off or broken? Is the tree healthy? Are the roots deep or shallow?

In addition to the general associations, certain species of trees carry their own meanings. Bristlecone pines speak of longevity and endurance. Oaks are sturdy and strong, sacred in Celtic traditions, symbolic of masculine strength, thunder and sky gods in others. The laurel is symbolic of triumph and victory, as a crown of laurel was a symbol of victory for ancient Greeks and Romans, awarded to athletes or military victors. Apple trees evoke both temptation (the tree of the Knowledge of Good and Evil in the Garden of Eden) and fecundity (Johnny Appleseed). Aspens remind me of subconscious connections and the interconnected web of existence, since whole groves of aspens can be one organism.

Tree imagery appears in our language: "can't see the forest for the trees," "up a tree," "money doesn't grow on trees," and "barking up the wrong tree." If one of these idioms comes up in association with the dream tree, it's worth pursuing its meaning further.

Even more specifically, a tree may have special meaning for the dreamer. I can't consider cottonwoods and weeping willows without thinking of my childhood home. For me, the willow is also a symbol of enduring love, as the giant in the family yard provided the backdrop for my sister's wedding. Like all dream symbols, when trees appear they bear multiple meanings, and it's always worth exploring whether the archetypal associations resonate with the dreamer, as well as pursuing more personal associations with trees.

Turtles and Tortoises

A giant tortoise once appeared in my dream, the same night two foxes were hanging out with my cat. The tortoise part of the dream was just a snapshot—it sat in my back yard. My waking life association with giant tortoises is that when I was a kid I got to ride one at the Lincoln Zoo. I know that they can live to a very great age, and I recently talked to a woman who has custody of one that she fully expects to outlive her.

One metaphorical association with turtles and tortoises is that they carry their homes with them, and so are, in essence, always at home. Their appearance in a dream reminds me that this is one of my lessons, to be at home within myself, within the present moment, and to shed the illusion that divine resides somewhere other than within.

Of course, there's also the fable of the tortoise and the hare, which teaches that "slow and steady wins the race." This is a comforting premise for me, for I tend to be slow and steady in my progress toward my goals (with the occasional exception for National Novel Writing Month, when I churn out 50,000 words in 30 days).

I also have a personal association with turtles as an example of a beloved pet, which is often a symbol for unconditional love. We had a box turtle named Charlie when I was a kid, which lived in a baby washtub and one day got lost. We'd searched everywhere, and finally my intuition led me to push down the pedal on the pump organ. Charlie had climbed the pedal, his weight enough to press it down so that he could slide off the other side into the cavity behind it, at which point the pedal rose to its usual position. So for me, turtles are also connected to my family role as "the finder," which is one of the ways my intuition expresses itself.

Twelve

Note: I posted this on my First Church of Metaphor website on December, 12, 2012.

Twelve disciples, things sold by the dozen, twelve signs of the Zodiac, twelve months of the year, twelve hours on the face of a clock—we have a lot of twelves in our cultural associations. But the deeper meaning of the number itself eluded me, beyond a sense of "coming of age," which much literature associates with twelve (the beginning of puberty) and again with eighteen (the end of puberty).

In *The Illustrated Encyclopaedia of Traditional Symbols*, J.C. Cooper states that twelve is the number of cosmic order:

"As 3X4 it is both the spiritual and temporal order, the esoteric and exoteric. There are the twelve Signs of the Zodiac and months of the year, of which there are six male and six female; twelve hours of the day and night...there are also the twelve days of return to chaos at the Winter Solstice, when the dead return, celebrated by Saturnalia in Rome and the twelve days of Yuletide and Christmas; these celebrations are also found in Vedic, Chinese,

Pagan and European symbolism. The days are said to forecast the meteorological pattern of the twelve months of the coming year."[23]

Because a twelve-sided figure approximates a circle, twelve is also a sign of completion and wholeness. Perhaps on this day of twelves, we can take stock of what's completed, what's whole. As I write this, the Mayan calendar is nearly at an end, so there is a lot of talk about endings and completion right now. Perhaps it's fitting that we have the reminder, before the "end of the world," that we're really just finishing one cycle and beginning another. Of course, depending on where you start counting, you're always at the end of a cycle and beginning another. It's just that sometimes, for whatever reason, our collective imagination fixates on the idea that one era is ending, and a new one is on its way. Let's pray that the coming world has more conscious awareness, more compassion, and more equality than the one we're leaving in the past.

Urine

One very common dream is of needing to find a place to pee. Jeremy Taylor's experience of working with this symbol in any number of clients' dreams is that it very often carries the meaning of needing to authentically express oneself. Of course, the dreams often correspond to a real physical need, but other dream symbols can also wake us up if the physical situation is urgent. So rather than dismiss

---

[23] Cooper, *The Illustrated Encyclopaedia of Traditional Symbols*, p. 120.

the dream as "only" the body's attempt to wake the dreamer, it's worth considering whether there's a place in the dreamer's life where authentic self-expression is being denied. After I took an opportunity to present my potentially unpopular opinion to a large audience, I had an intense dream of having urine coming out my mouth, which I took as an affirmation of how important that expression had been.

But I've also dreamed several times of animals urinating on me. I've been peed on by a wolf, a squirrel, and a butterfly in my dreams. I understood the dreams to suggest a kind of territorial marking, especially when it was the wolf and the squirrel. As a metaphor, then, these energies within me that look most like a wolf or a squirrel are claiming me as their own. I suppose the butterfly dream could be read the same way, but butterflies aren't known for marking territory the way wolves and squirrels do.

At the same time, I read these dreams as those energies needing to express themselves. They get my attention in no uncertain terms, and yet the dreams aren't nightmares, so the need for expression isn't as intense or urgent as if there were a lot of fear associated with them.

So what to do with a dream that encourages authentic self-expression? Sometimes writing a letter that I'll never send, and may even burn after writing, is enough. Sometimes I'm being encouraged to try a new art form, or to communicate something difficult to someone. Maybe all I need to do is dance. Whatever I choose to do, when I have a dream where I really need to pee, there's always an invitation to get my innermost thoughts out in some way.

Whales

Whales, as the largest mammal, and also very intelligent mammals, are complicated dream symbols. They are apparently conscious and self-aware, and they swim in the ocean, which is often associated with the unconscious. For me, that suggests that they come in dreams as reminders to expand conscious awareness. They communicate through vocalizations that sound to us more like song than speech, so if a whale shows up in my dream, it might come to remind me to sing or use music to get closer to spirit. If a whale breaches in my dream, it could be a suggestion to take a creative leap, to bring something out of the depths and into the world.

One of the archetypal whale stories in Judeo-Christian culture is the tale of Jonah, from the Old Testament, who was sent by God to Nineveh and when he tried to go instead to Tarshish, a great storm endangered the ship he was on and the sailors cast him overboard, which calmed the storm. Then Jonah was swallowed by the whale (or great fish, but in modern society, it's usually a whale) for three days before being spit out on land again. After that, Jonah obeyed God's command. The belly of the whale is, metaphorically, a kind of death, and Jonah's escape a rebirth. But there is more to the symbolism. When we are called, by whatever we name the divine creative power of the universe, we must answer or our lives become a kind of death, dark and unpleasant. So for me, a whale in a dream, most especially if I see the whale's belly, is a reminder that I should be doing my true work in the world.

(See also "Penguin and Whale")

Windows and Glass

Windows show up regularly in the dreams I have and those I hear from others. Usually the reference is to looking through a window and seeing something on the other side. Having heard these dreams worked in groups, there is often a layer of meaning that the dreamer understands a certain situation or problem from an intellectual perspective, but hasn't yet taken it in emotionally. This makes sense to me because if there's a layer of glass between myself and an object, I can view it, but not experience it through touch, or feeling. In this case, if I dream of shattered windows or glass that's generally a sign that I've understood the situation in a more emotional way.

Glass is a curious substance that doesn't fit with comfortable categorization. It's actually a liquid, which is why very old glass gets wavy and sags so that the bottom of a pane is thicker than the top. So even when I look through glass at something in my dream, there's the potential for that barrier to flow away. And since, in waking life, I look at the world through glass all the time, (I wear corrective lenses), glass for me is a symbol of how my point of view is shaped and brought into focus.

Windows can also represent my general outlook on the world. If in the dream I'm looking into a backyard, that might be a clue that I'm glimpsing something that has been unconscious. If I'm looking out over a grand view, my dream might be giving me a larger perspective. I also have to mention the phrase "windows on the soul," which is usually a metaphor for the eyes. In dreams, windows do indeed give me a glimpse into my soul.

Wolf

One of my friends reported, "I dreamed a lot about wolves after 9/11, and I never had before. But that's pretty obvious." Not having the narratives of those dreams handy, my guess is that the wolves appear as threatening, symbols of viciousness and appetite that could be associated with the attackers in the events of 9/11. As the Taschen *Book of Symbols* notes, "Particularly in Christian iconography they are the rapacious spoilers of sheep-like innocence."[24] Witnessing the deaths of innocent people would naturally bring such a predator to mind in a dream.

But I already know the obvious, that after the attacks I felt that innocence had been betrayed. I don't need my dreams to tell me that. Instead, the dreams offer this image, which in my imagined version carries overtones of a nightmare, in order to make sure I'm paying attention. After all, I can't easily forget a nightmare, and so

---

[24]*Book of Symbols,* p. 274.

the symbols linger longer than the ones from a pleasant or neutral dream might. So what other associations could the dream be offering to deepen my understanding of the attacks on American civilians?

It helps to remember that the wolves in these dreams are also symbols of me, the dreamer. They may represent my own desire for revenge, carefully shrouded from my civilized view of myself, the urge to take my pack with me to attack the attackers. But when I step away from the ancient human fear of the wolf, I can also see the animal's positive qualities. The pack is a network of support, in which the young are cared for by several adults and loyalty to the community is evident—in this sense the wolf represents my community, and so shows up in my dreams after 9/11 to remind me of what is good and important in my life. My community expanded after 9/11 to include sympathizing people from all over the world, and in those displays of support I found enormous comfort.

The system of establishing a pecking order in a wolf pack offers a symbol, as Ted Andrews suggests in *Animal Speak*, of expressing strength without resorting to violence. "Often a glance, a posture, a growl is all that is necessary to determine dominance....The Wolf teaches you to know who you are and to develop strength, confidence and surety in that so that you do not have to demonstrate and prove yourself to all."[25] If the attackers had had that inner strength, their attacks would have been unnecessary.

In my imagined version of wolf dreams, all these levels come into play: Family, government, community, loyalty, give and take,

---

[25] Andrews, *Animal Speak,* p. 324.

and strength without unnecessary violence. Imagining dreaming of wolves after 9/11, I can't escape the thought that times of crisis tend to unite communities, and that the dreams would be suggesting building on that community to create a more balanced world.

Further Reading and Links

The following list is by no means a comprehensive bibliography of work available on dreams, intuition, oracles, or any other aspect of the Invisible Realm. Almost all of the following are from my personal library, and are works that I have found particularly helpful in my journey.

On the Afterlife

Alexander, Eben. *Proof of Heaven*. Simon & Schuster, 2012.

Sudman, Natalie. *Application of Impossible Things: My Near Death Experience in Iraq*. Huntsville, AR: Ozark Mountain Publishing, 2012.

On Astrology (recommended by Catherine Woods, Astrologer)

Fairfield, Gail. *Choice-Centered Astrology: The Basics*. Weiser Books, 1998.

Bloch, Douglas, and George, Demetra. *Astrology for Yourself: How to Understand and Interpret Your Own Birth Chart*. Ibis, 2006.

McEvers, Joan, and March, Marion D. *The Only Way to Learn Astrology: Volume 1: Basic Principles*. Revised 2nd Edition, Starcrafts LLC, 2008.

Spiller, Jan, and McCoy, Karen. *Spiritual Astrology: A Path to Divine Awakening*. Revised Edition, Touchstone, 2010.

On Dreams

Bulkeley, Kelly, and Bulkley, Patricia. *Dreaming Beyond Death: A Guide to Pre-Death Dreams and Visions*. Beacon Press, 2006.

Bulkeley, Kelly. *An Introduction to the Psychology of Dreaming*. Praeger; Seventh Printing edition, 1997.

Epel, Naomi. *Writers Dreaming: William Styron, Anne Rice, Stephen King and 23 Other Writers Talk About Their Dreams and the Creative Process*. New York: Carol Southern Books, 1993.

Mellick, Jill. Foreword by Marion Woodman. *The Art of Dreaming: Tools for Creative Dream Work*. Berkeley, CA: Conari Press, 2001.

Moss, Robert. *Conscious Dreaming: A Spiritual Path for Everyday Life*. Three Rivers Press, 1996.

Moss, Robert. *Dreamgates: Exploring the Worlds of Soul, Imagination, and Life Beyond Death*. New World Library, 2010.

Moss, Robert. *The Secret History of Dreaming*. New World Library, 2010.

Moss, Robert. *The Three "Only" Things: Tapping the Power of Dreams, Coincidence & Imagination*. New World Library, 2009.

Taylor, Jeremy. *Dream Work: Techniques for Discovering the Creative Power in Dreams*. New York/Mahwah, NJ: Paulist Press, 1983.

Taylor, Jeremy. *The Living Labyrinth: Exploring Universal Themes in Myths, Dreams, and the Symbolism of Waking Life*. New York: Paulist Press, 1998.

Taylor, Jeremy. *"What Was That All About?" A Comic book About Dreams & What They Mean, With Special Emphasis on Projection.* Published under the auspices of Dream Tree Press, The Human Universe Foundation, and the Marin Institute for Projective Dream Work. http://www.blurb.com/b/1233477-what-was-that-all-about

Taylor, Jeremy. *Where People Fly and Water Runs Uphill.* New York: Warner Books, 1992.

Taylor, Jeremy. *The Wisdom of Your Dreams.* (Updated and expanded edition of *Where People Fly and Water Runs Uphill.*) New York: Jeremy P. Tarcher/Penguin, 2009.

Taylor, Kathryn. *Dreaming While I'm Awake.* Fairfield, CA: Dream Tree Press, 2009. http://www.blurb.com/b/750331-dreaming-while-i-m-awake

Dream Symbol Dictionaries

Andrews, Ted. *Animal Speak: The Spiritual & Magical Powers of Creatures Great and Small.* Woodbury, MN: Llewellyn Publications, Thirty-first printing, 2005.

Bethards, Betty. *The Dream Book: Symbols for Self-Understanding.* Petaluma, CA: Inner Light Foundation, 1983.

Cirlot, J. E. *A Dictionary of Symbols.* 2nd Edition. Translated from the Spanish by Jack Sage, Foreword by Herbert Read. Mineola, NY: Dover Publications, Inc., 2002.

Cooper, J. C. *The Illustrated Encyclopaedia of Traditional Symbols.* London: Thames & Hudson, Ltd., 1978.

Ronnberg, Ami, Editor-in-Chief, and Kathleen Martin, Editor. *The Book of Symbols.* Cologne, Germany: Taschen, 2010.

On the I Ching:

Wilhelm, Richard. Translated by Cary F. Baynes. Foreword by C. G. Jung. *The I Ching or Book of Changes*. Bollingen Series XIX. Princeton University Press, 1950.

On Intuition and Telepathy

Sheldrake, Rupert. *Dogs that Know when their Owners are Coming Home*. Crown Publishing Group, 2011.

Sheldrake, Rupert. *The Sense of Being Stared At and Other Unexplained Powers of Human Minds*. 3rd Edition. Inner Traditions/Bear & Company, 2013.

Sheldrake, Rupert. *Seven Experiments that Could Change the World*. Inner Traditions/Bear & Company, 2002.

On Metaphor and Symbolism:

Jung, C. G. *Flying Saucers*. Translated by R. F. C. Hull. New York: MJF Books, 1978.

Man and His Symbols. Edited, with an Introduction by Carl G. Jung, New York: Dell Publishing, 1964.

On Poetry

Luterman, Alison. "Written on the Bones: Kim Rosen on Reclaiming the Ancient Power of Poetry," *The Sun Magazine*, December 2010, pp. 4-11.

On Scrying

Robinson, Karen:
http://www.angelfire.com/my/zelime/hand_scrying.html

On the Tarot and some favorite Tarot decks:

Arrien, Angeles. *The Tarot Handbook: Practical Applications of Ancient Visual Symbols. Tarot Symbols from a Psychological, Mythological, and Cross-Cultural Perspective*. New York: Jeremy P. Tarcher/Putnam, 1997.

Baron-Reid, Colette. *Wisdom of the Hidden Realms*. Hay House, 2009.

Holloway, Sage, and Skaggs, Katherine. *Mythical Goddess Tarot*. Star Chalice Sisters Publishing, 2008.

Lehman, Connie, and Clurman, Irene. *Tarot Life Cards.* Connie Lehman and Irene Clurman, 2012.

Lösche, Norbert. *Cosmic Tarot*. F.X. Schmid, 1988.

Osho, and Deva, Padma. *Osho Zen Tarot*. St. Martin's Press, 1994.

Marchetti, Ciro, and Moore, Barbara. *The Gilded Tarot*. Llewellyn Worldwide, 2004.

Robbins, Morgan. *Morgan's Tarot Deck*. New York: U. S. Games Systems, Inc., 1983.

Websites and Links

Kelly Bulkeley: http://kellybulkeley.com

Laura K. Deal: http://www.lauradeal.com
http://www.firstchurchofmetaphor.org
http://www.thewildwriters.com

Brenda Ferrimani: http://www.brendaferrimanidreamart.com/
http://dreamingglobalillumination.com/

Robert Moss: http://www.mossdreams.com

Marcella Moy: http://www.inspirationist.com/

Billie Ortiz: http://www.wakeuptoyourdreams.com

Karen Robinson: http://www.angelfire.com/my/zelime/home.html

Suzanne Rougé: http://www.hummingbirdhorizons.com/

Rupert Sheldrake: http://www.sheldrake.org

Natalie Sudman: http://www.nataliesudman.com/

Mike Tappan and Irene Clurman: http://www.dreamportrayal.com/

Jeremy Taylor: http://www.jeremytaylor.com

http://www.psychologytoday.com/blog/the-wisdom-your-dreams/201101/eating-in-dreams

http://www.radiolab.org/2007/sep/24/behaves-so-strangely

http://www.radiolab.org/2007/sep/24/sound-as-touch/

http://www.sheldrake.org/Articles&Papers/papers/telepathy/babies.html

Acknowledgments

I offer profound thanks to Marcella Moy for suggesting that I write this book. The vision she had about its creation has manifested in unexpected and interesting ways. We found each other through the magic of dreams, meeting at one of Jeremy Taylor's weekend workshops at the Caritas Spiritist Center in Boulder, Colorado. The reading she gave me that planted the seed of this book took place at one of Billie Ortiz's dream work retreats, fondly known as Dream Camp.

The road that led me to that weekend started when I met Jeremy and Billie in 2000 at a workshop at Naropa University. Billie created her weekend retreats with Jeremy following a dream, and over the years, she built a family. I count myself fortunate to have had so many opportunities with Billie and Jeremy and my beloved dream family to sit in circles and immerse ourselves in the language of metaphor for a weekend. The gifts of healing that I have received in those and other dream circles are impossible to number, and they continue to unfold and offer me blessings. To all of you who have read dreams with me, or engaged in dream work with me through email, I offer thanks, because we've walked in many shadowed places and emerged more whole for having walked there together. Your compassion has held me together in the tumult of life over and over.

Even before I studied dreams, I knew I wanted to be a writer. Without my beloved writing friends, I'd never have endured the long years of honing my craft. I am thankful for my critique groups, Uff da Cum Laude, and the Wild Writers. The "Uff das" held my hand through every rise and fall of the rollercoaster ride and read everything from my poetry to my dissertation. The Wild Writers, with their extensive expertise, taught me an amazing amount about writing fiction and non-fiction and about navigating the writing life. Every writer should be lucky enough to have a critique group she can rely on to be supportive and honest, and I am blessed with two.

Thanks to my families, including the one I grew up in, the one I married into, and the "Walker Ranchers," who love me no matter what.

My biggest debt of gratitude goes to my husband, Kevin, and my daughters, Maia and Brenna, who made room in our life together for me to pursue my passions, and believed in me even in those times when I no longer believed in myself. You have always been my anchor and my most cherished reminder of what matters most in this life. I'm eternally grateful.